RECREATION MINISTRY
a Guide
for All Congregations

BILL MANESS

John Knox Press
ATLANTA

To Jackie with love

Library of Congress Catologing in Publication Data

Maness, Bill.
  Recreation ministry.

  Bibliography: p.
  1. Recreation in church work. I. Title.
BV1640.M36 1983   259'.8   81-85324
ISBN 0-8042-1186-8

John Knox Press
Atlanta, Georgia 30365

PREFACE

Recreation has made a significant impact on the church in the last decade. It has, in fact, become an integral and harmonious part of the total ministry of many churches. As a result, ministers and laypeople in churches without recreation programs are beginning to think about "recreation." When they do, many questions are raised: Why should our church get involved in recreation? What kinds of programs should be offered? Who will oversee them? What will they cost? How will they be financed? What can we do if we don't have a "gymnasium?" If we decide to build a building, what should it contain?

This book provides answers to these and other questions that are inevitably asked when people begin to talk about a recreation ministry for their church. But, it contains more than answers. It is a comprehensive, practical guidebook to starting and implementing a church recreation program. Beginning with a philosophy of recreation, it then moves into the "how-to's" of church recreation: how to decide what kinds of activities and classes to offer; how to determine costs and set fees; how to find instructors, train coaches, recruit volunteers; how to put together an athletic program for adults and children; how to use existing facilities of the church and those available in the community; how to design, furnish, and equip a recreation building; how to set up operational policies, schedules, and maintenance procedures when you move into a building.

The material is presented in such a manner as to enable the author and reader together to "think through" every facet of church recreation. In addition, this book discusses those persons who will ultimately bring about the recreation ministry, from the qualifications and responsibilities of the director (or minister) of recreation to the selection and role of the recreation committee.

This book should be a valuable tool in the hands of the student who is *studying* recreation, the layperson who is *considering* a recreation program for the church, and for the minister who will be *implementing* a church's recreation program.

FOREWORD

I am happy to write a word introducing the author of this volume. Bill Maness is one of those remarkable individuals who combines a strong commitment to Christ and the church with a multiplicity of talents. He has created at the Peachtree Presbyterian Church in Atlanta a unique program of recreation which combines the fundamentals of good sportsmanship and faith. It is a program that reaches a variety of people and involves them in meaningful relationships while at the same time emphasizing physical fitness and tension-releasing fun.

More than 2,000 people a week move through our program, and it has become an increasingly meaningful part of our church's ministry to its own family and to the community at large. It is something that any church, regardless of size, can do, so I not only commend this volume to you but recommend its careful study.

W. Frank Harrington
Atlanta, Georgia

CONTENTS

1

PHILOSOPHY:
Recreation in Perspective

When I became recreation director at Peachtree Presbyterian Church, my first task was to address the congregation. Our Family Center was nearly complete. A recreation director had been hired. It was appropriate at that time, I thought, to put it in perspective, to answer the question: "What is the recreation ministry at Peachtree going to be like?"

It was a question I had been asking myself. I found the answer in two passages in the book of Psalms: *recreation at Peachtree is for the renewing of the spirit and making glad the heart.* In Psalm 51:10, David pleads for forgiveness and cries, "renew a right spirit within me" (KJV).

We pronounce it *recreation* because we soften the "e," but the word is actually "rēcreation." The word comes from the verb "to rēcreate." It means: to create anew, to make over, to restore, to renew. It is essentially the same word used in Revelation 21:5 in which Christ says, "Behold, I *make* all things *new*" (author's italics). The Greek word is *kainos,* which means "to restore, to refresh, to renew, to recreate." It is not a chronological word; it does not mean to make "brand" new. Rather, the word has to do with "quality." It means to restore something to its original quality — to take something old and worn out, and make it like new again.

Inherent in God's "creation" is the potential for "rēcreation." All of nature testifies to that fact. Our oft-sung hymn, "Morning Has Broken," recounts that truth in the last verse:

Praise with elation;
Praise every morning.
God's rēcreation
Of the new day.*

But rēcreation is not limited to nature; it can happen in people. We read with dismay reports in the daily papers of the increasing use of drugs and alcohol. Commenting on the situation, a noted Atlanta psychiatrist has stated, "People are under a lot of pressure these days — they work long hours under trying circumstances which leave them exhausted, and most of them don't know how to recharge themselves. Consequently, they resort to drugs and alcohol."

But their spirits are not renewed. And that's what the ministry of church recreation is all about. It's for the renewing of the spirit. Recreation in the church is more than playing on a basketball team, learning how to square dance, finding out how to bid a bridge hand, discovering that you can pick out a tune on a guitar, toning muscles in an exercise session, or creating something pretty in a crafts class. Rather, it's that intangible something that takes place inside an individual as a result of having done these things. It's that recharging of the body, that restoring of the mind, that renewing of the spirit. So, recreation at Peachtree is, first of all, for the renewing of the spirit.

Psalm 122:1 is a verse that every child in Sunday school can recite: "I was glad when they said unto me, 'Let us go to the house of the LORD.'" It seemed to me that our Family Center, which would soon be the focal point of our recreation ministry was as much the "house of the Lord" as was the first house of the Lord — the temple built by King Solomon.

Whereas Solomon's temple was fashioned from timbers cut from the cedars of Lebanon, our Family Center was constructed with bricks made from Georgia red clay. But it's no less the house of the Lord. Solomon's temple was overlaid with gold; our Family Center is overlaid with epoxy paint, but it's no less the house of the Lord. We don't have a court of the priests; instead we have a gymnasium and a game room. We don't have candlesticks and an ark of the covenant; instead, we have basketball goals and ping-pong tables. But, it's no less the house of the Lord.

And it should be a place where people are glad to come, to play together, to exercise, to work with their hands, to have fun and fellowship. It should be a place where children squeal when they shoot a basket; where parents cheer, regardless of the score; where players shake hands, and even hug one another, when the game is over. It should be a place where smiles are abundant, laughter is loud, and joy is contagious. It should be a place where new friends are made, faith is shared, and Christ is proclaimed. It should be a place where families and teenagers and children and the elderly will say, "I was glad when they said unto me, 'Let us go to the house of the LORD.' "

And so, that is what recreation at Peachtree is like. It is for the renewing of the spirit and making glad the heart.

Recreation in the Church

Why does recreation enjoy such a harmonious relationship with the church? Perhaps it is because of its two-fold nature: it is both *nurturing* in its essence and *evangelistic* in its appeal. It is in this dual role that recreation has found a home in the church.

One of the responsibilities of the church is to nurture the children of God — to provide the stimuli for their growth in Christ. Recreation is one such stimulus. Paul speaks of the fruits of the Spirit as being: love, joy, peace, longsuffering, gentleness, goodness, faith, temperance. What better way is there for church members to develop and learn to apply these virtues than through recreational activities. Recreation can, indeed, be a vineyard in which such fruit can be cultivated, nourished, and ultimately harvested.

Another reponsibility of the church is evangelism, and recreation can be an instrument for evangelism. First of all, recreation obviously appeals to the personal interests of many individuals. They participate in recreation activities for any number of reasons: they like competitive sports, they want to learn new skills, they are looking for creative ways to spend leisure time. It is not surprising that Jesus appealed to the interest of those he sought when he said to a band of fishers, "I will make you fishers of men." It is appropriate, therefore, that the church should offer recreation because it appeals to the interests of many. Evangelism begins when you get someone's attention, and recreation is an attention-getter.

Secondly, recreation is an invitation to come to church. When Philip became a disciple, he told Nathanael, "We have found Jesus of Nazareth." Nathanael's response was, "Can anything good come out of Nazareth?" to which Philip answered, "Come and see." Recreation is, in a way, an invitation to many to "come and see" what our church is all about. There are many who don't go to church and may not have been in years. There are many unsaved who have no need for church and would not darken its doors were it not for an invitation to "come and see" couched in a softball application form. But the initial appeal and the invitation are only the beginning of evangelism. Once you've gotten someone there, what then? Don't think that because someone is playing softball one day, he or she will join the church the next. While this does happen, it is the exception to the rule. The rule is that evangelism occurs in direct proportion to the effort made in its behalf.

What happens to those individuals who register for softball and are put on a team? Will the recreation director call them to find out if they go to church, whether or not they are Christians, whether or not one of the ministers can be of help? Do the members who are on the team invite the non-members to Sunday school and to worship with them in church?

The church should remember that it is not primarily in the business to provide recreational activities. If recreation is seen as an entity, in and of itself, then it has lost its purpose. Recreation in the church should be conceived in terms of a means, not an end. If the purpose of it all is to play softball and learn to square dance and make quilts, then it is nothing more than any other recreation "program" run by a local municipality. It becomes a "ministry," however, when it is seen in perspective, as a tool for the implementation of the gospel and the uplifting of Christ.

OPPORTUNITIES AT PEACHTREE

SUNDAY MORNING WORSHIP SERVICES - 8:30-11:00 a.m.

Dr. W. Frank Harrington and our other ministers lead us in worship through meditation, sharing, illumination and service.

"You enter this church, not as a stranger, but as a guest of Jesus Christ"

A delayed telecast of the 11 o'clock service may be seen at 7:00 p.m. on WHAE-TV, Channel 46.

SUNDAY SCHOOL - 9:30 a.m.

Fifteen different classes for adults, offering a variety of subjects for men, women, couples and singles, as well as classes for children of all ages.

YOUTH FELLOWSHIP - Sunday evenings, 6:00-9:00 p.m.

High school youth practice their Christian faith through programs, recreation, retreats and week-long Camp Rutledge.

PEACHTREE CONNECTION - Wednesday evenings

Meets from mid-September through mid-May

Youth Club - 4:30-6:30 p.m.

Our Christian education program for children in the first through seventh grades, featuring Bible study, music and recreation.

Supper - Served from 6:15-7:00 p.m.

Bethel Bible Series - 7:30-8:30 p.m.

A two-year overview of the entire Bible.

H.E.L.P. - 7:30-8:30 p.m.

A variety of classes to "Help Equip Lay Persons" for Christian service. Includes in-depth Bible study, Christian beliefs, issues in Christian living, and "how to" minister to others.

MUSIC

Choir programs for all ages

4 & 5 year olds - Wednesday afternoons, 5:30 p.m.
Grades 1-7 - Wednesday afternoons, 4:30 p.m.
Grades 8-12 - Sunday afternoons, 5:00 p.m.
Adults - Thursday evenings, 8:00 p.m.
Handbells - Contact Minister of Music for rehearsal schedule.

RECREATION

Sports

Basketball for men and women
Softball for men and women
Volleyball for men and women

Arts, Crafts & Hobbies

A variety of classes and activities offered throughout the year.

Fitness

A year-round fitness program for women with both morning and evening classes.

Youth

Basketball for boys and girls, ages 7-18

Basketball Camp for children

P.L.A.Y. - Planned Leisure Activities for Youngsters, a summer recreation program for children.

"Be a Sport" - pre-athletic training for young children.

WOMEN OF THE CHURCH

Service, witness, worship and growth opportunities for women. Day circles meet at 10:30 a.m. on the first Tuesday of each month; evening circles meet at 6:30 p.m. on the second Tuesday.

PEACHTREE OUTREACH PROGRAM

Our weekday kindergarten for underprivileged children

WEEKDAY KINDERGARTEN

A program of early childhood education combining high professional standards with Christian nurture. For children two through five years of age. Weekdays from 9:00 until 12:00 noon.

VACATION CHURCH SCHOOL

A program of Christian nurture and training for children. One week each August.

PEACHTREE FELLOWSHIP

Retirees meet once each month for programs of fun and fellowship.

MEN'S PRAYER BREAKFAST

Men meet for worship every other Friday morning at 7:11 a.m.

BOY SCOUTS

Troop No. 34 meets every Monday evening at 7:30. For boys 11 through 15 years of age.

COUNSELING CENTER

Counseling by appointment for individuals, couples and families, as well as group workshops.

AFFILIATION

Peachtree Presbyterian Church extends an invitation to you to join by (1) profession of faith in Jesus Christ as the Son of God and Saviour of sinners; (2) Re-affirmation of your faith if you are not now active in a Christian church; (3) transfer of your letter from another Christian church.

One of our ministers would be delighted to talk with you about these and other opportunities at Peachtree. Call us at 261-7651 and let us share our Christian experience with you.

2

PROGRAM:
Classes and Activities

Once you've decided to have a recreation ministry, the next question to consider is "what kind?" Having determined that, you'll need a plan for implementing it. In this chapter, we'll explore the *what?* and *how?* of programming.

Determining What to Offer

What will your recreation ministry consist of? Will you have exercise classes for women? A jogging program for men? Soccer for children? Will you offer family camping? Will you promote backpacking trips? What about square dancing, bridge, creative writing? Will you have a softball team that plays in a church league, or will you form your own league? A good place to begin is to find out what people want. You do that by asking, and you ask by conducting a *survey.* Then, you'll need to consider the *facilities and equipment* available to you. The "space" you have and how it is furnished will affect your capacity for programming.

And, you'll want to explore the *financial implications* of each class and activity. Some classes have the potential for "making" money; others "cost" money.

A SURVEY — DETERMINING WHAT PEOPLE WANT

A successful recreation ministry is one that meets the needs and interests of a church's members and those of the community it serves. One of the most reliable means of finding out what people want is through a survey in which they are asked to indicate their interests. A questionnaire (similar to the sample Interest Survey) could be sent to each family in the congregation. Within a week or so, you would have a good idea of where their interests were.

Or, you can get an immediate and almost one hundred percent response by distributing the survey during the Sunday school hour, allowing a few minutes of class time for filling it out. When you do this, however, you should be sure to send one to those who don't attend Sunday school. Recreation may be the area in which they will begin to become active church members.

With the responses in hand, you'll be ready to begin outlining your program. When the surveys are returned, a composite list can be made. From it you can readily determine where interests lie. This should be your first step in deciding what programs you will offer. Notice in the sample questionnaire that persons are asked to check not more than three activities in each category. You will get a more accurate reading this way than if you had them check "everything" they were interested in.

Remember that a survey does more than measure interest. For one thing, it can turn up leadership for your programs that you otherwise might not be aware of. Therefore, include a space where people can note those areas in which they can "lead." A file of this information will be invaluable when you begin looking for teachers, coaches, and volunteers. Secondly, a survey gives each member of the congregation an opportunity to get involved in the planning stages of your ministry. By responding to the survey, they, in effect, adopt it as their own.

You will likely want to modify our sample so that it will reflect your thinking. Be sure to include instructions for returning the survey when it is completed. Once you know what your people want, then you're ready to consider what programs you *can* offer as determined by your facilities and equipment.

11

RECREATION MINISTRY
INTEREST SURVEY

A separate survey should be completed by each family member. In each category, please check no more than *three* activities in which you would likely participate. Check *all* activities in which you could give leadership.

Name _____ Age _____ Sex _____ Date _____

Address _____ City _____

Zip _____ Home phone _____ Office phone _____

Sunday school class _____

	Interested In	Could Lead		Interested In	Could Lead		Interested In	Could Lead
ARTS, CRAFTS, & HOBBIES			Fashion & Beauty	__	__	**PHYSICAL FITNESS**		
			Other	__	__	Women's exercise	__	__
Bridge	__	__	Specify _____			Men's exercise	__	__
Ceramics	__	__				Co-ed exercise	__	__
Flower Arranging	__	__	**OUTDOOR ACTIVITIES**			Jogging	__	__
Calligraphy	__	__	Family Camping	__	__	Yoga	__	__
Quilting	__	__	Hiking	__	__	Weight control	__	__
Home Landscaping	__	__	Fishing	__	__	Bicycling	__	__
Needlework	__	__	Canoeing	__	__	Other	__	__
Specify _____			Other	__	__	Specify _____		
Vegetable Gardening	__	__	Specify _____					
Flower Gardening	__	__				**YOUTH**		
Water Color Painting	__	__	**TABLE GAMES**			Tumbling	__	__
Oil Painting	__	__	Pool	__	__	Gymnastics	__	__
Gourmet Cooking	__	__	Bumper pool	__	__	Fitniks	__	__
Microwave Cooking	__	__	Ping-Pong	__	__	Day Camp	__	__
Amateur Radio	__	__	Chess	__	__	Other	__	__
Home Repair	__	__	Other	__	__	Specify _____		
Photography	__	__	Specify _____					
Square Dancing	__	__				**SOCIAL**		
Ballet	__	__	**SPORTS**			Covered-dish dinners	__	__
Modern Jazz	__	__	Softball	__	__	Family night events	__	__
Collecting	__	__	Basketball	__	__	Picnics	__	__
Specify _____			Soccer	__	__	Other	__	__
Rug Hooking	__	__	Tennis	__	__	Specify _____		
Basketry	__	__	Golf	__	__			
Leather Craft	__	__	Badminton	__	__	**VOLUNTEER SERVICE**		
Metal Craft	__	__	Volleyball	__	__	Receptionist		__
Specify _____			Rollerskating	__	__	Secretary		__
Woodworking	__	__	Bowling	__	__	Committee		__
Model Railroading	__	__	Other	__	__	Officiating		__
Guitar	__	__	Specify _____			Specify _____		

COMMENTS: Please indicate other activities you would be interested in which do not fit in the categories above. In addition, would you share any thoughts you have regarding our recreation ministry.

_____

_____

_____

FACILITIES AND EQUIPMENT

Your facilities and equipment (or those you plan to build or purchase) will determine, to some extent, the programs you will be able to offer. (See chapters 7 and 8.)

To play volleyball, you not only need an area big enough for the court, you also need twenty feet of unobstructed space *above* it. Some fellowship halls are suited for volleyball; others are not. On the other hand, there may be an ideal spot on your parking lot to play volleyball.

A tumbling class for small children can be done in almost any large size room, if you have gym mats. If you go further into a bonafide gymnastics program, you'll need additional equipment (beam, horse, parallel bars, safety mats, etc.), all of which is expensive, cumbersome to move, and requires extensive space for use and storage.

A bridge class requires card tables; they are relatively inexpensive. A ceramics class, on the other hand, requires a kiln, which is costly both to purchase and to operate.

Rollerskating is a popular family activity. But you'll find yourself spending several thousand dollars if you try to buy enough skates for a dozen families.

As you can see, the classes and activities you can offer are limited by the facilities and equipment available to you. With a little ingenuity, however, you can do a lot with what you have and what may be available to you if you look around.

In chapter 8 on *Limited Facilities,* I suggest doing an inventory of your current space and furnishings. At some point in your planning, you'll want to prepare such an inventory, even if you have a well-equipped recreation facility. You'll need to have the inventory at hand in order to determine what programs you *can* offer. Once you've determined the facilities and equipment available to you, then you're ready to look at the financial considerations.

INCOME VS. EXPENSE

There are two ways to finance a recreation ministry: you may allocate a certain amount of your church's budget to underwrite the cost (or most of it) of the recreation ministry, or you may operate on the basis that the recreation ministry will support itself as far as direct costs are concerned. (See chapter 5.)

For the sake of illustration, let's assume the latter to be the case. If that is so, a class' or activity's potential for producing revenue versus the anticipated cost of offering it is a factor to be considered in planning your recreation program. In that regard, it is the *pupil/teacher ratio,* everything else being equal, that most directly affects the income vs. the cost of a class. (See chapters 3 and 5.) An exercise class, for example, in which an instructor can teach up to forty or more pupils, will bring in proportionately more in relation to the cost of the instructor than a ceramics class in which the teacher must spend time with each student, and, therefore, may only be able to work with ten students at a time.

Exercise, square dancing, bridge, and ballet classes, for example, can be effectively taught to large numbers of people at a time. Guitar, needlepoint, water color painting, and flower arranging, on the other hand, must be kept small so that the teacher can devote adequate time to each student.

A couple of examples will illustrate this: An exercise class with thirty students, each paying $20.00 for a course that meets sixteen times (two times a week for eight weeks) will produce an income of $600.00. An instructor making $20.00 per class times sixteen classes would receive $320.00 The net income to the recreation ministry would be $280.00. A guitar class with ten students each paying $25.00 would bring in $250.00 If the instructor were paid $30.00 per class for eight classes ($240.00), the net income would be $10.00.

But consider this. What if only nine persons enrolled for guitar lessons? Or eight? What would you do? Would you cancel the class after those eight had made arrangements to participate, perhaps having bought a guitar in anticipation of learning to play it? You might renegotiate the salary arrangements with the instructor who may be willing to take less in this case. (It's not a bad idea to have discussed this possibility at the time the instructor was secured.)

On the other hand, if you offered *both* classes — guitar *and* exercise, the income from both would be sufficient to pay both instructors. We'll have more to say about this in chapter 5 on *Financing* and in chapter 3 on *Staff.* Suffice it to say at this point that by offering some classes which have a high income to expense ratio (pupil/teacher ratio), your surplus from those classes will enable you to also offer many classes which will not produce any income above cost — and may actually "lose" money. By doing so, you will be able to present a variety of activities which will meet the needs of many different people and still operate on a favorable financial basis.

I have listed a number of popular classes according to their pupil/teacher ratio. This ratio is usually determined by asking the instructor how many pupils he or she can comfortably handle and still accomplish the objectives of the class.

PUPIL/TEACHER RATIO
OF VARIOUS CLASSES

25+/1

Exercise
Bridge
Cooking (microwave or gourmet)
Square dancing
Rollerskating lessons

13-24/1

Calligraphy
Photography
Ballet
Golf lessons
Yoga

12 or less/1

Ceramics
Flower arranging
Quilting
Painting (water color or oil)
Needlework
Guitar
Tumbling
Tennis lessons

Remember, that while other factors, such as equipment and materials will affect the income vs. expense of offering classes, the primary element is the ratio of pupils to the teacher.

Implementing Your Program

When you've made the decision as to *what* to offer, your next concern is *how* to do it. We've divided this process into three steps: organization, scheduling, and registration.

ORGANIZATION

Specific activities and programs usually fall into a smaller number of general categories. We have grouped ours into five broad areas: Arts, Crafts, & Hobbies; Fitness; Youth; Sports (see chapter 6); and Special Events. Sometimes the placing of an activity into a group is not clear-cut. Youth basketball, for instance, would fit into either youth or sports. Some activities, on the other hand, don't fit neatly into any. We usually put them in the catch-all category of Arts, Crafts, & Hobbies.

Grouping not only provides a convenient means of keeping tabs on a variety of different activities, it is particularly helpful, as we shall see later, from the standpoint of budgeting. In this section, we'll look at each category and suggest some ideas for programming.

Arts, Crafts, & Hobbies

This division covers an assortment of classes and activities which involve working with the mind and hands,

learning new skills, making things.

Some of these activities provide sufficient instruction for the participant the first time around. That is, many find that one session of an art or craft, such as flower arranging, for example, gives them a level of knowledge and a degree of skill that is adequate for their purposes. We have found this to be true in such things as quilting, gardening, microwave cooking, etc.

On the other hand, many classes lend themselves to advanced instruction, as the student wants to go beyond the basics. Classes such as bridge, in which intermediate and advanced levels get into more sophisticated bidding and play; ceramics, in which students become more adept at working with clay and glazes; guitar, in which additional chords and picking techniques are learned; ballet, in which progressively more difficult positions are mastered should be considered.

Intermediate and advanced instruction in Arts, Crafts, & Hobbies classes should be considered if there is sufficient interest. Bear in mind, however, that attrition will occur; not everyone who takes the beginner class will enroll in the next level.

Fitness

Physical fitness classes are invariably popular, particularly exercise classes for women. You might even find interest in a men's early morning fitness class (combining calisthenics and jogging, with breakfast served afterward) or one for men in the late afternoon, that they could catch on the way home from work. Co-ed exercise classes in the evening are being well attended, and there is always interest in weight control classes which incorporate exercise and diet instruction. In addition, special exercise programs such as yoga and aerobic dancing have good participation.

Fitness classes, unlike Arts, Crafts, & Hobbies classes tend to be "continuous" in nature. Because fitness, once acquired, must be maintained, many of the participants in a given fitness class will continue to register for session after session, as long as they are pleased with the class. You'll find that many of the people in your fitness classes will be "repeaters."

Youth

Those activities specifically designed for elementary school age children come under our category of Youth. Tumbling classes, baton twirling lessons, "Be-a-Sport" (our pre-athletic skills program for 4- through 6-year-olds; described in this chapter), "Afterschool" (our supervised "do-your-own-thing-in-the-gym" program for 7- through 10-year-olds) are examples.

P.L.A.Y.

P.L.A.Y. stands for Planned Leisure Activities for Youngsters. It's Peachtree's unique summer recreation experience for boys and girls 6 to 8 years of age.

In P.L.A.Y. children do things that are fun. They make their own fishing poles and actually go fishing in a pond stocked with bream. They make toys in the Toy workshop. They sing, and laugh, and play games, and learn about God.

Here's what a typical day consists of . . .

9:00	-	"Do your own thing" in the gym
9:15	-	"Get together" for singing, Bible lesson and sharing
9:30	-	Group time: 3 periods . . . Toy Workshop, games, funtime
11:00		Lunch
11:30	-	Quiet time: skits, stories, thinking games
12:00	-	Rollerskating, fishing, games
1:00	-	Movies and refreshments
2:00	-	"Busting loose" in the gym
2:30	-	Time to go

Activities and scheduling may vary from day to day.

P.L.A.Y. is directed by Lynn Hildreth. Staffed by Peachtree Presbyterian youth.

Each session of P.L.A.Y. will last for one week:

      1st session - June 16-20
      2nd session - July 7-11

Fee: $25.00 per week. A $10 deposit will reserve a place.

In addition, our summer day camp programs: P.L.A.Y. (described in this chapter), "Be-a-Sport" (day camp version), and Basketball Camp, fall into this category.

Special Events

Those one-of-a-kind activities such as the church-wide picnic or a family fun-run come under this "special" category. Your grouping will vary, but for organizational purposes, you will find it helpful to categorize your activities in some similar manner.

SCHEDULING

Scheduling is not only a matter of time and facilities, but of people. A recreation ministry will mean increased demands on facilities. Their use by recreation will have to be coordinated with that of the other ministries of the church. But, there will also be more opportunities for

"Be-a-Sport"

"Be-a-Sport" is Peachtree's own program of sports and exercise to develop the pre-athletic skills young children will need to participate in various sports: football, soccer, basketball, baseball, track, gymnastics.

Following the principles of "movement education," children learn in a non-competitive atmosphere of fun ... without the pressure to "perform."

In the process, movement is perfected, coordination refined. Muscles become stronger and more supple, running becomes faster, jumping springier, throwing farther, catching surer, kicking straighter, dribbling more controlled.

This "day camp" approach to "Be-a-Sport" has grown out of the success of our after school program this past year.

Directed by Lynn Hildreth. Assisted by Peachtree Presbyterian youth.

Each session will last for one week, meeting from 9:00 a.m. until 1:00 p.m.

> 1st session   -   June 23-27
>
> 2nd session   -   July 14-18

For boys and girls who are 4, 5 or 6 years old.

Fee: $25.00 per week. A $10 deposit will reserve a place.

---

people to participate in the life of the church. Coordination in this regard is essential, too, in order to minimize the conflicts that will inevitably occur when programs of two or more ministries take place at the same time. Scheduling, therefore, is not just listing times and places, it is the synchronization of activities into a harmonious ministry that will make the fullest use of space and also provide the greatest opportunity for participation.

Two examples will illustrate how we've worked through this process. Our square dance class was meeting in our fellowship hall on Tuesday evenings. Then in its fourth year, this established class had spawned a square dance club, many members of which were assisting with the class. Not long ago, one of our staff members wanted to begin a "singles" ministry one evening a week. As supper was involved, fellowship hall was the logical place (being next to the kitchen and large enough to serve the group), and Tuesday night was the only practical night. To have asked the square dance group to move would have been inappropriate, yet the potential for ministry with singles was apparent. We were able to solve both problems by asking the singles group to remove the tables after supper and the square dance group to begin a half hour later. This was not only the result of a cooperative spirit among the staff persons involved, but also, and equally important, among those affected by the problem.

In another instance, the games in our men's softball league were scheduled for Monday and Thursday evening. Choir practice also took place on Thursday night. Our choir director was concerned that several men in the choir who were not yet "committed" to the choir had indicated to him that they wanted to play softball during the season. We were able to put all of the choir members on the same team and arrange the schedule so that that team played all of its games on Monday nights.

Despite this kind of approach to scheduling, conflicts will occur. At some point it is inevitable that as your church programs expand, some persons will have to "choose" between two or more worthy activities. Regular and careful planning on the part of the entire church staff, however, will keep this to a minimum. With this in mind, let us take a look at scheduling for various elements of recreation: Arts, Crafts, & Hobbies; Fitness; Youth; and Special Activities.

Arts, Crafts, & Hobbies

Our Arts, Crafts, & Hobbies classes are presented four times a year, coinciding with the seasons. Our fall program begins in late September (after children have returned to school, and things are back to normal) and runs through November. The winter session goes from early January through early March; spring, from late March through late May. Our summer session, offered on a smaller scale than the other sessions, runs from mid-June through mid-August. We have found participation to be the greatest in the winter, when there's less to do outside. Fall and spring enrollment is somewhat less; summer enrollment is considerably less.

Each session we offer those standbys which have a proven track record. Then we add a sprinkling of others that are appropriate for the season, for instance, those involving "making things" are popular during the fall session when people are thinking about Christmas presents; microwave cooking always goes in the winter when homemakers are wanting to learn how to use the ovens they received at Christmastime.

We have found that *eight* weeks is about right for most Arts, Crafts, and Hobbies classes. That allows us to fit each session into a season and still have a two to three week breather in between to get ready for the next session. Some classes are longer than eight weeks; some shorter. Square dancing is taught in two fifteen week periods — part I in the fall, part II in the winter and spring — to accommodate the requirements for certification in that activity. We run quilting for four weeks, the class on college board preparation for six, the pilot training class for ten. The instructor usually has a recommendation as to how long the course should be if eight weeks is out of the question. Eight weeks, on the whole, however, has proven about right for us. People seem to be willing to commit themselves to a two-month period of time.

Most of our classes last about an hour and a half, although there is flexibility here, too. Guitar and ballet go for an hour, bridge is an hour and twenty minutes, college board prep lasts two hours. Again, as with the number of classes, I discuss the length of each class with the instructor, and we decide together on what seems appropriate. In most instances, we offer both morning and evening classes. The morning classes are usually attended by housewives, those in the evening by working men and women.

Fitness

Women's exercise classes are the most popular activity we offer. Morning classes which usually meet three times a week (Monday, Wednesday, and Friday) are taught as early as 8:30 A.M. so that mothers driving their children to school can drop by for exercise before returning home. An additional class is taught at 9:30 for homemakers who want to straighten the house a bit before exercising. A third class, which meets around 10:30, is designed for older persons and those who have not exercised regularly and need an "easier" class.

Evening classes are always full. We teach them two nights a week (Monday and Thursday). Our first class at 6:00 P.M. is primarily attended by working women who catch an hour of exercise on the way home; our 7:00 P.M. class is the favorite of working mothers who have to prepare supper before going out to exercise.

To facilitate publicity and registration, our Fitness classes follow the fall, winter, spring, summer pattern, beginning the same weeks as our Arts, Crafts, & Hobbies classes. Because of the continuous nature of exercise, however, we either make them longer (ten to twelve weeks) to fill up the interim between the end of one eight week session and the beginning of another, or we offer a "mini-class" which runs for the duration of the interim. The latter has worked well with us. We simply prepare a flyer announcing the "mini-class" and pass it out among those participating a couple of weeks before the class is scheduled to end. Those who want to continue return it with the fee — which has been prorated for the length of the interim.

Youth

During the school year, youth activities are generally possible only in the afternoon. Children in kindergarten and first grade can usually make a 2:30 or 3:00 P.M. starting time. Older children's activities may have to begin around 4:00 or 4:30 P.M. Check with the schools in your area to find out what time children in each grade are dismissed. Remember, in scheduling, they will need to get from school to the church.

We follow the same eight week schedule for our youth activities, however, classes are usually only forty-five minutes to an hour in length, depending on the age of the children participating. Our summer programs usually are of the "day camp" type. The age of the children dictates the programming for each day. A look at the description of our P.L.A.Y. and "Be-a-Sport" programs will give you some ideas of what has worked for us.

Special Events

Special events — picnics, retreats, campouts, overnight outings, trips — need special scheduling. Before any scheduling of special events is done, two sources of information are essential. First of all, you'll need a school calendar for each of the school systems in your area. Any activity involving school age children will have to fit into school schedules. You'll need to know when school begins, when it ends, the dates for holidays, Christmas recess, spring break, mid-term and final exams. If possible, try to secure similar information on the colleges and universities where you have students. A general idea of when quarters or semesters begin and end will be helpful in planning for this age group. In addition, if you live in a city where college or professional sports are played, it would be a good idea to have those schedules at hand.

Once the information on school dates and sporting events has been entered into your calendar, then you are ready to begin the planning of your special events. Special events should be planned a minimum of six months in advance; a year is better. All such planning should be done in consultation with the entire ministerial staff. Once your scheduling has been done, it should be entered into a year-long calendar of all church activities. Include the beginning dates of each session of classes, summer day camp weeks, and special events.

REGISTRATION

When you have determined, scheduled, and publicized what your program will be (see chapter 4 on Publi-

city), you are ready for people to register for it. Before registration takes place, however, you will need a plan for registering. In this section, we'll suggest some procedures that will facilitate the registration process.

How Will People Register?

Registration for classes is usually handled through one or more of the following methods: *in person, by mail,* or *over the phone.* We'll look at the pros and cons of each.

Registering *in person* has several advantages: (1) registrants can ask questions and get immediate answers; (2) specific information (such as a list of supplies that will be needed) can be given out. (In addition, general information about the other programs of the church can be given out as well. See our "Opportunities at Peachtree" brochure at the end of this chapter. We give this to every person who registers in person.); (3) payment of fees can be made; (4) an excellent public relations opportunity is afforded.

The disadvantages of registering in person are: (1) someone, either a volunteer or paid staff person (or persons) must be present during the entire time; (2) if registration is likely to be heavy, special days and times must be set up for this; (3) at peak registration times, people may have to stand in line before they can register, (4) if people have many questions, or have not filled out the application form, or do not have the correct payment, additional time will have to be taken.

Registration *by mail* has some distinct advantages: (1) the applicant can fill out a form giving the necessary information; (2) payment can be enclosed; (3) there are no lines to stand in; (4) the registrations can be processed by a paid or volunteer secretary in the quiet of an office during slack periods.

The disadvantages of registering by mail are: (1) questions cannot be asked or answered; (2) information cannot be given out, except by return mail, which is costly and time consuming; (3) there is no opportunity for positive public relations.

Registration *by phone* has the following advantages: (1) it is convenient for the registrant, who does not have to make a trip or send in a form; (2) questions can be asked and answered; (3) information (about what to bring, etc.) can be given over the phone; (4) there is some possibility for public relations.

The disadvantages of phone registration are: (1) no form has been filled out (it may have to be filled out by the secretary); (2) it ties up the phone, which means many people will have difficulty getting through to register, *and* the phone lines will not be available for other church business; (3) no payment of fees has been made, which means that the registrant may not show up for class after all; therefore, there is no way to know for sure how many will actually participate.

Our procedure for most recreation classes is to register persons both *in person* and *by mail*. In person registration is taken during regular office hours. In addition, if a class is not full, a person may register with the instructor when he or she comes to the first class.

While we do not accept any phone registrations, we do let persons who have waited till the last minute to inquire know whether or not there are still openings in the class in which they are interested, and whether or not they may come to the first class and register with the instructor.

The Application Form: Having the registrant fill out an application form is essential if you are to have good registration procedures. A copy of our typical form shows the information we request: Class (or Activity), Day(s) the class meets, Time, Fee, Participant's name, Age (if child), Address, City, Zip, Home and office phones, Parent's name if class is for child, Church affiliation, and Nursery information. There is also a box for our use.

Our application forms are 4"x6" so they will fit into a standard file box.

Handling Application Forms: We prepare a tabbed index card for each class during a given session and file the forms accordingly. Before filing, the secretary notes: the date received, the amount paid, and her or his initials. In addition, in the top right-hand corner a number is placed representing the order in which the application was received. By filing the cards in reverse order, we can immediately see how many have registered for each class.

Receipts: We do not normally give receipts for payment, unless they are requested. Receipt forms should be available, however, for those who pay cash in person.

Class Size (Maximum/Minimum)

Before registration begins you will need to determine the limitations of class size—the minimum and the maximum number of participants. These decisions are usually made with the instructor at the time he or she is secured. (This process is discussed in detail in chapter 3 on Staff.)

First-Come-First-Serve: Acceptance of registrants is usually handled on a first-come-first-serve basis. Members are given priority in registering in that they receive the publicity a week or so before non-members.

Waiting List: In every instance, when a class fills, a waiting list is prepared. It may be that there is sufficient interest to warrant an additional class. If that is the case, we contact the instructor to see if another class can be set up.

If Class Has to Be Cancelled or Is Full: Persons who register by mail are notified by mail if a class has had to be cancelled due to insufficient enrollment or if it is filled to capacity. The accompanying form illustrates

---

RECREATION AT PEACHTREE

Class (or Activity) _____ Day(s) _____ Time _____ $ Fee _____

Participant's Name _____ Age (if child) _____

Address _____ Home Phone _____

City _____ Zip _____ Office Phone _____

Parent's Name if Class is for Child _____

Church Affiliation _____

Nursery needed for

Name _____ Age _____

FOR CHURCH USE:

Date Received _____

Please return this form along with your check to:
**Recreation Ministry, Peachtree Presbyterian Church
3434 Roswell Road, N.W., Atlanta, Georgia 30305.
Telephone 261-7651**

PEACHTREE PRESBYTERIAN CHURCH
3434 Roswell Road, N.W.
Atlanta, Georgia 30363

Dear Parent:

We're delighted that your child will be participating in our
_____ P.L.A.Y. program _____ Basketball Camp beginning _____
morning, _____ at 9:00 a.m.

Please plan to have him (or her) here no earlier than 8:55. You
can drop your child off at the entrance to the Family Center that is under
the covered walkway. One of our counselors will be there to greet the
children upon arrival.

Please pack a sack lunch. Be sure to put the child's name on the
sack and indicate whether it should be placed in the refrigerator. We
will provide fruit juice or other drinks at lunchtime, and we will also
provide refreshments in the late afternoon.

The children can wear any kind of comfortable play clothes and shoes.
(Basketball campers should wear basketball or tennis type shoes.) All
activities will be over at 3:30 for P.L.A.Y. and 4:00 for Basketball.
You should plan to pick your child up at that time.

According to our records, you: _____ have paid in full; _____ have
paid $10.00 deposit and owe a balance of $15.00 which should be sent to
us by return mail. Make checks payable to: Peachtree Presbyterian Church
and mail to P.L.A.Y. (or Basketball Camp) at the above address.

We look forward to providing a meaningful summer experience for
your child. If you have any questions, don't hesitate to give us a call.

Sincerely,

Bill Maness

Bill Maness

M/p

our means of doing this. If there is not time to notify them by mail, we give them a call.

Additional Information

Sometimes it is necessary to give out additional information which could not be included in the original publicity. An example of this can be seen in the form sent to the parents of children who register for our P.L.A.Y. program and Basketball Camp. The form indicates when the child is to arrive, where to go, what clothing is appropriate, when to be picked up, any balance due in fees, etc.

Confirmation

We do not send out any confirmation of acceptance when an application is received by mail, except when additional information is required as indicated above.

Rejecting Applications

In order to assure quality in programming, all of our classes are limited in size. We have found that people often do not understand why "just one more" person cannot be enrolled. We explain that for the sake of those who registered in time, we cannot take any more in that class, and that we will be glad to place their name on a waiting list, in case an opening occurs.

Class Rosters

A class roster should be prepared for each teacher, listing the students' names and phone numbers. The teacher should call the roll to verify that each student has, in fact, registered.

Using the suggestions outlined above, you should be able to set up workable procedures for registration.

Peachtree Presbyterian Church
3434 ROSWELL ROAD, N.W.
ATLANTA, GA. 30363

Thank you for your interest in our recreation program. Regretfully, the class you have registered for . . .

_____ has been cancelled due to insufficient enrollment.

_____ is full (your name and phone number have been put on a waiting list and you will be contacted should an opening occur or a new class be offered.)

_____ Your check is enclosed.

_____ As your check has already been deposited, we will send you a refund in a few days.

If you have any questions, please don't hesitate to call us at 261-7651.

                    Bill Maness
                    Director of Recreation

3

STAFF:
Leadership for Your Program

Your program will rise or fall on the quality of leadership it has. In this chapter, we'll talk about your staff — those persons who will teach, lead, and/or direct the activities in your program. They are the ones who will most directly determine how good your program is. While it may look great — may meet the needs of persons, may be competitively priced, may be effectively publicized — its ultimate success will be measured by the leadership you have provided for it. It is the person who is up in front of the class who will be the basis on which your program is judged.

We have found that leadership within a recreation ministry falls into three distinct areas: *teachers,* who are usually already qualified to teach a particular class; *volunteers,* who need to be trained to lead in particular activities; and part-time paid staff persons, who supervise the building, particularly during afternoon and evening hours. Coaches will obviously play a major leadership role in your program, but we will reserve discussion of coaching to the chapter on Sports.

Teachers

Most of your classes and activities will have to have teachers. Generally speaking, teachers are already equipped to teach. Unlike volunteers, teachers will come with the essential skills and knowledge in their field so that they are already qualified to go to work for you. You would expect, for instance, that a square dance instructor would know "squares" and calls, a guitar instructor should be able to teach chords and strumming techniques; a photography instructor should be able to define terms such as focal length, ASA, and f. stop. Your primary responsibilities as far as teachers are concerned, therefore, are "finding" and "hiring."

FINDING TEACHERS

Once you've determined which classes you will want to offer, your next step is to find teachers for them. Where do you look? Most of our teachers have come from four areas: within the church, hobbyists, school teachers, and professionals.

Church Members

Remember your survey? If you've done your homework, you should have a file of potential teachers made up of those members who indicated an interest in leading various recreation activities. There may be a young person who would like to teach a ladies' exercise class, an individual who has skills in needlepoint to share, an avid fisher who would love to teach a class in fly tying and casting. The information from your survey should provide you with a number of promising leads.

You should be aware at this point that there is a potential problem with using church members as teachers. What if you and your committee feel that a particular member who wants to teach a class is not qualified? What if two different members want to teach the same class and one is obviously more qualified than the other? How will you explain to a member that you do not have a position open or that you have chosen someone else?

I believe the best approach is to begin by writing each person who indicated an interest in leading and asking them to send you a brief resume. In fact, you might even send them a form to fill out, specifically requesting such information as: educational background, qualifications, teaching experience, etc. That way, you will have something in writing on which you and your committee can make a decision. In addition, those who are not qualified are not as likely to pursue teaching any further.

Hobbyists

Persons with hobbies frequently make good teachers. A numismatist may want to teach a class in coin-collecting, a ham radio operator may teach amateur radio, a model railroader a course in model railroading. Hobbyists are usually qualified by virtue of the time and interest they have put into their hobby. They may not be as professional as one who is in the business but they often impart an enthusiasm for their subject that a professional does not have. Once your program is established, hobbyists will contact you, wanting to teach their avocation. Some will want compensation; some will teach for free. Occasionally an instructor may simply want to use some of your equipment in return for teaching — for instance, a ceramics instructor may be willing to teach if she or he can fire some pieces in your kiln.

School Teachers

School teachers often make excellent teachers in a recreation ministry. A high school teacher came to me one day with the idea of teaching a class to prepare high school students to take the college board exam. We offered it and it has been one of our most popular courses ever since. This same teacher happened also to be an assistant football coach. He suggested a class for women on the basics of football. His class which deals with equipment, plays, positions, the playing field, offensive and defensive patterns has made Monday Night Football at least "passable" for many women.

Physical education teachers are particularly good with young children's classes in fitness and sports activities. We have used them frequently for our tumbling, "Fitniks," and "Be-a-Sport" programs.

Professionals

If I were going to offer a winter class in beginning golf in our gym, I would talk to a local golf pro. Last year we had two classes learning to hit golf balls into nets strung the length of our gym. The golf pro was able to teach the basics of the golf swing in the warmth of a gym when it was too cold outside for anyone to be playing.

If you wanted to offer a course in backyard vegetable gardening, why not contact a local nursery? Want to have a photography course? Find a professional photographer. Many professionals in their field make their living as teachers, e.g., a golf pro. Many may have never

taught, e.g., a professional photographer. Having taught before is not necessarily a prerequisite for being a good teacher. Having knowledge or a skill that you want to share is.

On the other hand, when talking to a professional, note that some have a vested interest in what they are teaching. I would prefer, for instance, to have a professional photographer teaching a photography class than a professional who owns or operates a camera store. The latter may be inclined to do more "selling" than "teaching." Once you've found the teacher you want, your next step will be to hire that person.

HIRING TEACHERS

You may occasionally be able to find teachers who will donate their service to the church. More often than not, however, they will want to be compensated for their time and talent. In that case, how much should a teacher be paid? The "going" rate at the time this book is being written is around $20-$25 per class. For a course that contains 8 classes, a teacher makes $160-$200. With inflation, it will likely be higher by the time you read this.

A teacher's salary is also tied into the fees that participants will have to pay to take the course and the number of students that can effectively be taught in it. I once had an art instructor who was willing to teach for what I thought was a fair salary, but when we began discussing the number of students she could handle, she wanted to limit the class to a maximum of six — preferably four or five. She was used to teaching only two or three at a time in her home and did not feel that she could effectively work with ten or twelve. Limiting the class to such a small number would have required unreasonably high fees for each student, so I looked around for another instructor.

In negotiating a teacher's salary I use a formula which puts both the salary and the fees for the class in perspective. The formula is based on the principle which we have adopted as a budgetary guide (see chapter 5 on Financing.) in which we pay an instructor no more than 60% of the total income received. The remaining 40% is used to cover other expenses: publicity, materials, equipment, secretarial services, etc.

The formula begins with a suggested rate of pay for the instructor. That figure is multiplied by the number of classes to be taught to determine total salary. The salary is then divided by 60% (.6) to determine the income that we will have to receive in order to pay that salary. Then by dividing the income by the minimum number of students anticipated, we come up with a fee for the class. If the fee looks reasonable, we go with it.

The formula is:

$$\frac{}{\text{Rate}} \times \frac{}{\substack{\text{\# of} \\ \text{Classes}}} = \frac{\$}{\text{Salary}} \div .6 = \frac{\$}{\substack{\text{Income} \\ \text{Needed}}} \div \frac{}{\substack{\text{Minimum} \\ \text{Enrollment}}} = \frac{\$}{\text{Fee}}$$

The following example will illustrate my procedure for determining salaries and fees: recently I talked with the pastor of a small local church whom I had learned was a writer and also taught a class in creative writing. I was interested in having him teach a course for us.

I knew from his resume that he had authored several books and many articles, and that he had conducted creative writing workshops in a number of colleges. Based on his credentials, and in light of what we usually pay instructors, I felt his request of $30.00 per class was not unreasonable.

Using the formula above, I determined the fee as follows.

$$\frac{30^{00}}{\text{Rate}} \times \frac{8}{\substack{\text{\# of} \\ \text{Classes}}} = \frac{\$240}{\text{Salary}} \div .6 = \frac{\$400}{\substack{\text{Income} \\ \text{Needed}}} \div \frac{16}{\substack{\text{Minimum} \\ \text{Enrollment}}} = \frac{\$25^{00}}{\text{Fee}}$$

The formula simply serves as a guide for reconciling the salary and fee. The "variables" in the formula — that is, the number of classes and the minimum expected enrollment should be decided in consultation with the instructor. It is the instructor who can best decide how many classes are appropriate and will probably have some idea as to the minimum number that could be expected.

What if the minimum number is not reached? What if, in the creative writing class mentioned previously only twelve had enrolled? That would mean that the income would be only $300. In that case, I would probably call the instructor and tell him or her the situation. Hopefully, we could agree on a compromise, say, $200 for the teacher, $100 for the church. I inform all instructors before we sign a contract that this is a possibility, so I have already set the stage for this, should it occur. On the other hand, if more than the minimum enroll, the balance goes to the church.

What would I do if only eight enrolled for the class? In that case, the total income would be only $200. I would probably offer the instructor $175 (or perhaps all of the $200) so that the class would "go" for the sake of the students. This could be done because other classes which exceed the minimum would generate sufficient extra income to cover indirect expenses.

For each class, we prepare a worksheet (see accompanying example) in which we record such information as the name of the class, when it is to begin, the name, address, and phone numbers of the instructor, the days and time the class is to be held, the length of the class, the rate of pay, the number of classes, the class size (maximum and minimum), and the formula (mentioned earlier). At the bottom of the worksheet, we can record the gross income less the salary and the resulting net to the recreation ministry. These worksheets are kept in a notebook for each series of classes that we offer.

The maximum enrollment is determined by mutual consent. The instructor usually has an idea as to the maximum that one can teach effectively. When that number is reached, enrollment is closed.

A "contract" is prepared and signed by each instructor. The contract outlines the responsibilities of both the instructor and the church. The contract also classifies the instructor as an "independent contractor" and not an "employee" of the church. It is not necessary to withhold social security and income taxes from the money paid to an independent contractor.

At the time the contract is signed, I find out from the instructor what equipment will be needed (projector, blackboard, phonograph, etc.) and how the room should be set up as far as tables and chairs are concerned.

Volunteers

The church is a place for service. Those with melodic voices sing in the choir. Those with a gift of teaching teach Sunday school. There are many members of your church, however, who would feel out of place singing in the choir or would balk at the idea of teaching a Sunday school class. A recreation ministry opens a whole new area of opportunities for those who want to serve but have not yet found their niche in the other activities of the church.

Many volunteers, while they may be eager and enthusiastic, will need to be trained to serve. Unlike teachers who are already qualified, most volunteers will not be. That's where you come in. Volunteers will provide you with an unparalleled opportunity to develop a leadership team. Volunteers, in this regard, take more time and energy on your part than teachers. But you will have the grand responsibility for the "equipping of the saints for the work of the ministry."

In this section, we'll look at recruiting, training, and supervising both adult and youth volunteers.

ADULTS

Usually, though not always, adults are more willing to commit themselves to specific, short-term projects,

CLASS WORKSHEET

CLASS _____ TO BEGIN _____

INSTRUCTOR _____

ADDRESS _____

HOME PHONE _____ OFFICE PHONE _____

* *

$$\underset{\text{Rate}}{\underline{\hspace{2cm}}} \; X \; \underset{\substack{\text{No. of}\\\text{classes}}}{\underline{\hspace{2cm}}} = \underset{\text{Salary}}{\underline{\hspace{2cm}}} \div .60 = \$ \underset{\substack{\text{Income}\\\text{needed}}}{\underline{\hspace{2cm}}} \div \underset{\text{Fee}}{\underline{\hspace{2cm}}} = \underset{\substack{\text{Minimum}\\\text{enrollment}}}{\underline{\hspace{2cm}}}$$

1st class   _____

        Day   Time   Salary

2nd class   _____   _____   _____

3rd class   _____   _____   _____

4th class   _____   _____   _____

TOTAL   _____

Gross income _____

less salary _____

Net income _____

PEACHTREE PRESBYTERIAN CHURCH
3434 Roswell Road, N.W.
Atlanta, Georgia 30363

CHURCH/INSTRUCTOR CONTRACT

Peachtree Presbyterian Church (hereinafter "the church") and the undersigned individual (hereinafter "the instructor") agree as follows:

1. The instructor will teach a course upon the subject, and on the dates and at the times and place, specified below:

Subject:_____

Dates and times of sessions:_____

_____

_____

Place:_____

2. Upon the completion of the course, the church will pay the instructor the amount of $_____.

3. The content of the course and the manner of teaching shall be within the control of the instructor, so long as the course is upon the subject above specified. It is the intent of the parties that the relationship between the church and the instructor shall be that of independent contractors, and the instructor shall not be an employee of the church in the performance of this contract.

4. The course will be made available to members of the church and, in the discretion of the church, may be made available to other persons. The church may make a reasonable charge to persons taking the course.

5. This contract is conditioned upon _____ persons signing to take the course.

Dated: _____19

Peachtree Presbyterian Church

By_____

_____
Instructor

rather than a perpetual activity. I have found that they respond better when they are volunteering for something that has an end in sight, for example, coaching a youth basketball team. Most of your adult volunteers will likely be involved in your athletic program as coaches and officials. We'll defer discussion of volunteer coaches and officials to chapter 6 on Sports.

Recruiting

Recruiting is often just a matter of letting people know that you need volunteers. Several months ago we ran this announcement in our bulletin:

> We're getting ready to have rollerskating for families on Friday nights. Before we do, however, we need eight families to serve as hosts — two families will be needed each Friday night per month. We will provide the training. If you can help, contact Bill Maness.

We not only reached our quota, we even began a waiting list of families that wanted to volunteer.

Sometimes, however, it is not that easy. Potential volunteers may need a little more prodding. You may have to use the typical approach of a first sergeant, "Smith and Jones, I want you to volunteer for patrol duty." This is not a bad idea in that it allows you to be selective in recruiting. You will find persons whom you might want to do a particular job. Ask them. Don't be timid. Some of your best leadership will come from persons who have to be convinced they are needed. After all, Nathanael had to be persuaded to become a disciple.

One of the primary responsibilities of a recreation director is recruiting volunteers. I suggest that you begin to cultivate a list of prospective recruits. Look for leadership qualities in individuals as they participate in your activities. You'll be amazed at the leadership that you'll turn up among your members. And, you will have done them a great service when you recognize their potential and help them to nurture it.

Training

Once recruited, most volunteers will need to be trained. Training may be a simple process. Take the rollerskating hosts, for example. My training session for them consisted of a Sunday afternoon meeting in which we reviewed procedures for opening and closing the building, turning lights on and off; we formulated rules for skaters; we discussed basic skate maintenance (how to tighten and/or loosen wheels and trucks, how to replace toe stops, how to re-tip laces, etc.); we made assignments for the first month of skating; and we set a date to get back together and see how everything was going after a month's experience.

A month later we met again. At that time we devised a procedure for letting the volunteer in charge of skate repair know which skates needed work and what was needed, and we determined that we needed to order more skates of a particular size.

Other training may be much more involved. Getting a volunteer ready to coach a youth basketball team is more complicated. (We'll discuss that process in chapter 6 on Sports.) Nonetheless, training will be one of your primary responsibilities as a recreation director. I believe that you will make one of your biggest contributions to a recreation ministry through your recruiting and training of volunteers, for it will be through the volunteers that you train that you will have the greatest impact on the lives of others.

Remember, not all volunteers, however, will have to be trained. You may find a golfer with experience in tournaments to help you set up your annual golf outing. A certified referee may help with the training of officials for youth leagues. There will always be a need for persons to help with banquet decorations, the annual picnic, etc. Keep your eyes open for people that you can enable to become volunteers.

YOUTH

Teenagers are always full of energy and ideas. Your job will be to channel their vigor and inventiveness into avenues of productivity. We have found that young people work better in a "club" setting. At the outset of my ministry, I conceived the idea of a corps of high school students who would volunteer their time and talent to the church through the recreation ministry.

They came to call themselves the "Gym Team" because they were the team of volunteers that worked in the gym. A letter, sent to prospective members, explains the concept and organization of the Gym Team.

Recruiting

Recruiting is not a problem. The Gym Team is so much fun for the members that rising ninth graders are waiting in line to join. At this point, the process becomes one of selection, and that usually takes care of itself when the youngsters begin contemplating the commitment they will have to make. While the Gym Team is not an exclusive group (anyone who is a member of the church is welcome), I personally encourage some to join whom I have seen demonstrate leadership potential in other youth activities.

Dear _____

Perhaps you've already heard something about the Peachtree
Gym Team.

The Gym Team consists of twenty or so young people like
yourself (in the 9th through 12th grades) who volunteer their
time serving their church through its recreation ministry.

They work with the Youth Club program, conducting recreation
activities for 1st through 7th graders, they officiate at
youth basketball games, during the Bethel Kids Time, they
skate on the skate patrol, show movies, monitor in the study
hall, keep the control counter and equipment room in order.

As you can see, being on the Gym Team will require work,
but you won't be doing all of these things. You'll get to
choose one or two that you'd really like to do, be trained
to do them, and you'll be responsible for getting the job
done that's assigned to you. There'll always be another
Gym Team member working along with you, and you'll always
be under the direction of a member of the recreation staff.

I know that many of you will be busy this year with school,
extracurricular activities, and other church responsibilities,
but if you have an average of one day a week to spend, I
think you'll find the Gym Team an exciting, challenging,
and rewarding way to spend it.

We're going to have an organizational meeting on Tuesday,
September 5th, at 7:30 in the Youth Lounge. It won't be
a long meeting, but I would like to go over all the details
of the Gym Team with you and answer any questions you may
have. Let me know by Sunday if you can come.

Thanks,

Bill Maness

Bill Maness

Training

Gym Team training begins with a lock-in on a Friday night in September. During the afternoon and early evening, we review the various activities with which the Gym Team will be responsible. Before they go to bed that night, they will have learned how to conduct games for children of different ages, their duties when on skate patrol, how to operate a movie projector.

The lock-ins are not all work. We stay up late — playing and laughing together — but by morning, all, including the new recruits, feel a part of the "team" and know where they're supposed to be, when they're supposed to be there, and what to do when they get there. Those who complete their training are given a team uniform which they are expected to wear when they are on duty. The uniforms add to the *esprit de corps* and identify them as leaders. During the year, the Gym Team takes two trips together — one ski trip and one beach trip. While each member pays his or her own way, the trips are made in recognition of service throughout the year.

Two things have contributed to the successful use of high school students as volunteers. Being a part of a team effort has given each a sense of identity, and adult supervision has given direction to their energy. As a result, the members of our Gym Team not only render a valuable service to their church, but have each experienced personal growth as they have learned to minister to others.

Part-time Paid Staff

We hire part-time employees to work at our control counter during the afternoons, evenings, and Saturdays when the Family Center is open. High school students usually work the afternoon shifts (3:30-6:00 P.M.); college students the evening shift (6:00 P.M. until closing).

Their primary responsibilities, depending on what happens to be going on while they're on duty, include supervision of building operation, coordination of evening activities, distribution of athletic equipment, registration of participants for classes, and answering the phone. Specific duties are outlined in the list of procedures that follows:

CONTROL COUNTER PROCEDURES

Opening
1. Screw down panic bars on glass doors (side entrance) so they will not lock when closed.
2. Turn on appropriate lights for areas to be used. (Refer to schedule of activities.)
3. Thermostats generally should not be adjusted unless absolutely necessary. The heat should be set on 68° and the air conditioning should be set on 78°.
4. Turn on gymnasium exhaust fans if needed. In hot weather the rear and front gym doors may be opened to increase air flow in the gym.

Closing
1. Turn off all lights (upper and lower lobby lights will remain on).
2. Secure latches on metal doors at rear of gym and at bottom of each stairwell.
3. Make sure craft room windows are locked.
4. Lock wooden doors in front of building.
5. Unscrew panic bars on glass doors so they will lock when closed.

Responsibilities
1. Ask to see the Activity Cards of those wishing to use the gym. Persons attending regularly scheduled classes for which they have already enrolled, and those attending special activities, e.g., Play Night, Youth Fellowship, etc., where there is an adult leader, need not show a card.
2. Persons who are not members of the church but would like an Activity Card should fill out the application form and return it along with the appropriate fee.
3. Check out equipment only to persons who have an Activity Card. Take their card when equipment is being used and return it when the equipment is brought back.
4. Check valuables by putting them in a numbered pouch. Keep valuables locked in the equipment room.
5. Keep the equipment room and control counter clean and orderly.
6. Keep an adequate supply of pens, note paper, and application forms for current activities at hand.
7. At 5:00 P.M., flip phone buzzer switches to "on." Answer phone by saying, "Peachtree Presbyterian Family Center; this is (your name)."
8. If an accident occurs, administer first aid and record victim's name, address, phone number, extent of injury, and how it occurred.
9. Do not permit unauthorized persons behind counter.

Building Supervision
1. Refreshments are not permitted in the gym. They may be taken to the classrooms by persons enrolled in classes.
2. Smoking is prohibited in the building.
3. Set up athletic equipment (volleyball nets, adjust backboards, etc.) as needed.
4. No dunking of basketballs is permitted.
5. Kicking of balls in the gym is prohibited.
6. Keep all storage room doors locked.

Coordination of Classes
1. Check with each instructor before class begins to see if room is properly set up and equipped.
2. Assist new participants in locating classrooms.
3. Register persons who want to enroll in classes if the classes are not already full.

General Instructions
1. Check your box in the secretary's office for messages and special instructions.
2. Leave messages for the director or secretary in appropriate boxes.

4

PUBLICITY:
Selling Your Program

Webster defines *publicity* as "information designed to attract public attention."

Publicity is the key to the success of your program. Regardless of how good your program is, people won't sign up for it if they don't *know about it.* Publicity is how you let them know about it. In this chapter, we'll look at publicity that just happens (word-of-mouth), the *elements of good publicity,* and the *production and distribution* of publicity.

Word-of-Mouth

There are two kinds of publicity: that which you produce and distribute, and that which happens as a result of people's reaction to your program. People's reaction manifests itself through that process called *word-of-mouth.* Whether you like it or not, it will be one of your most prolific kinds of publicity. Word-of-mouth can "make" or "break" your program, and there's not a lot you can do about it one way or the other. Your program, whether it is good or bad, is going to be talked about. If the talk is positive, you couldn't buy better advertising. If it is negative, all the advertising you could buy wouldn't help.

If you have a program that is meeting people's needs, one that is innovative, well-supervised, people are going to talk it up. And that kind of advertising, whether it takes place over the back fence, the phone, or a cup of coffee, is impossible to beat. No piece of printed material can equal the selling job of a satisfied customer. If, on the other hand, your program is tentative, unimaginative, and poorly administered (or if it is perceived to be that way), it won't take long for word to get around.

An example of how both good and bad publicity can result from word-of-mouth occurred in the same program at our church. Trying to find a creative program for young children, we came up with the idea of a class to teach kindergarten and first grade children some of the pre-athletic skills they would need to participate in the varied sports programs that would be available to them when they got a little older. We had a college athlete working for us at the time, so we developed a class called "Be a Sport." In it we taught five-and-six-year-olds such things as how to kick, throw, catch, dodge, strike, and dribble a ball, using the soft foam balls manufactured under the trade name of "Nerf." In addition, the children learned how to run, jump, tumble — the kinds of skills they would need later to play basketball, soccer, football, baseball, etc.

In a non-threatening, non-competitive atmosphere, the children responded beautifully. At the end of eight weeks, it was obvious to anyone who had seen them at the first class that they had progressed tremendously, not only in the development of physical skills, but in their self-confidence, as well. Obviously, word got out, for when we registered for the next eight-week period, we were inundated with requests. Despite the fact that we added more classes, we still had to turn away almost as many as we could take. Word-of-mouth had obviously had its impact.

At one point during the second eight-week period, however, the instructor called in sick. As it was too late to notify the parents that that day's class would have to be postponed, we simply put a sign outside the gym stating that the class had been cancelled and would be made up later. Unfortunately, we failed to indicate the reason — the teacher was ill. When the parents drove up and saw a birthday party taking place in the gym (which we had moved from another location, since the gym would be vacant) and the cancellation notice on the door, they incorrectly inferred that we had cancelled the class in deference to the birthday party. Within a matter of a couple of hours, word was going around that we did not have our priorities in order. It took several phone calls from my secretary in order to squelch that rumor.

You can count on word-of-mouth. While you don't have any direct control over what people say about your program, you can affect it indirectly by the program itself. That's why it's important to give adequate attention to details in the planning and implementation of your program. And remember, the way a person perceives your program to be is to that person the way it is. We'll have more to say in chapter 6 about the need to enlighten people about what you are doing.

Four Elements of Good Publicity

Now let's talk about the kind of publicity that you produce and distribute. This is the way you have of letting people know about your program.

To be effective, publicity must do four things:
1. It must get to the *right people.*
2. It must be *interesting* enough to get them to respond to it.
3. It must give them the *facts,* so they can decide whether or not they want to participate.
4. It must give them a *way to respond.*

1. GET IT TO THE RIGHT PEOPLE

The first thing to consider in planning your publicity campaign is *whom* you want to reach. Let's say you are going to offer a summer recreation program for young children. Where are the children now? They are in school. Doubtless, every child who would be eligible to respond is attending a school in your church's neighborhood.

Then why not prepare a flyer to be given out in the schools? (See "On Distributing Information in Schools" at the end of this chapter.) That way, you make direct contact with *the* audience you want to participate. The flyer containing the information about your program ends up in the hands of the persons you want to respond — in this case, elementary school age children. On the other hand, advertising such a program on a rock radio station, whose primary audience may be teenagers, would have little or no response.

If, however, you are having a class to help prepare high school students to take their college board exams, promoting it on a rock radio station may be the most ef-

HUCK FINN
Never Had It So Good!

Summer Fun for Boys & Girls
at Peachtree Presbyterian

Adults can have fun too!

fective kind of advertising, as it would be heard by those whom you want to sign up for the class.

To promote a volleyball league in which Sunday school classes compete against one another, go directly to the audience you want to reach — publicize it in your Sunday school classes. In addition, find someone in each class who likes volleyball and have that person not only promote it, but also be responsible for organizing a team from the class.

If your church wants to sponsor a high school basketball league, promote it in the high schools. A notice on a school bulletin board (be sure to get permission), an ad in a school newspaper, or an announcement over the public address system will get responses. Another approach is to ask the physical education teachers to distribute flyers to interested students. Most teachers will be delighted to promote any program that they believe will be beneficial to their students.

Well, you get the idea. Single out the audience you want to reach before you begin your publicity program. Then direct your publicity, both in content and distribution, to that audience. Remember, to be effective, publicity should be aimed at the right people.

2. MAKE YOUR PUBLICITY INTERESTING

Okay, you've decided the people to whom your publicity will be directed. Now, how are you going to get them to respond? A school child's response to a flyer may be to fold it into a paper airplane and toss it across the room. Or he or she may lose it on the way home. What will make a child look at it, read it if old enough to do so, and, in any case, make sure it gets into the hands of mom and dad with a "Can I do this?"

You appeal to children with pictures, color, big print. Take a look at the front of our flyer, "Huck Finn Never Had It So Good!" With a picture of Huck Finn and a fishing pole and a can of worms, we promoted our P.L.A.Y. (Planned Leisure Activities for Youngsters) summer program of fun for boys and girls. Since the program was a success from the start, we assume the flyer was interesting enough to get children to open it up and read about making a fishing pole and then going fishing with it in a pond stocked with bass and bream, and making a boat out of scraps of wood and then floating it down a creek, and "bustin' loose" in the gym each day — and excited enough to see that it got into the hands of someone who would make it all come true.

You appeal to adults in much the same way. The cover of a recent *Recreation at Peachtree* brochure contained a montage of pictures — people skiing, playing basketball, tumbling, playing volleyball, dancing — pictures of people having fun. Would you open it up if you received it in the mailbox along with three other pieces of third class mail? In many cases, I believe, one decides to participate in a church recreation activity, not because the individual was "looking for something" at the time, but rather because the person saw something that appealed to personal desires. Make your publicity interesting, and people will respond to it.

3. PRESENT THE FACTS IN AN ORDERLY MANNER

Once you've gotten their interest, what's next? Let's assume that your brochure on recreation at your church arrives in the mail. If it looks interesting, someone will likely read it. Perhaps over a cup of coffee at the kitchen table, a housewife may look it over. She'll glance from item to item until something strikes her fancy. It may be that "Ladies' Exercise" catches her attention. Maybe it'll be the "Fitniks" class for her four-year-old. When

RECREATION AT PEACHTREE . . .

Physical Fitness

YOGA EXERCISES **$20.00**
Relieve tension, experience true relaxation, improve flexibility. A co-ed class. Taught by Alice Stevens. Thursday mornings, 10:00-11:15 a.m. or Monday evenings, 6:45-7:55 p.m. (Beginner) or 8:00-9:10 p.m. (Intermediate)

LADIES EXERCISE

Calisthenics, stretching exercises and aerobic activities to improve muscle tone, flexibility and endurance. Performed to music.
Morning Classes (Taught by Dale Simmons) Monday, Wednesday & Friday, 8:50-9:40 a.m. or 9:15-10:10 a.m. **$24.00**
Beginner class for women who haven't been exercising regularly. Monday & Wednesday 10:15-11:00 a.m. **$17.50**
Evening Classes (Taught by Margaret McCamish) Monday & Thursday, 6:00-6:50 p.m. or 7:00-7:50 p.m. **$20.00**

"GETTING STRONG" **$15.00**
A weight training class (using common household items) for women who want to develop "shapeliness" (not bulky muscles) and strength in the upper body. A perfect complement to a "slimnastics" program. Six weeks. Taught by Alice Stevens. Monday. mornings, 10:15-11:00 a.m.

D.I.E.T. DIET INFORMATION & EXERCISE TRAINING

There are only two ways to lose weight: diet and exercise.
This class combines both in a sensible approach to reaching and maintaining your desired weight. Weekly weigh-ins. Four weeks. (Taught by Dale Simmons) Tuesday & Thursday mornings, 9:00-10:15 a.m. **$22.50**

Education

PLANNING FOR RETIREMENT

Retirement can be an exciting time . . . if you have planned for it. Topics include, psychological adjustment, housing, taxes, finances, legal aspect, second career, hobbies, travel, social security. Six weeks. Sue and Addley Gladden, coordinators. **$20/individual; $30/couple.** *Thursday evenings. 7:30-9:30 p.m.*

BREAKING INTO PRINT **$25.00**
Tools for those who want to be published and helps for marketing material. Taught by Cecil Murphey, who has 8 books in print and has published more than 75 articles in various magazines. He regularly teaches writing in colleges and workshops. Six weeks. Monday evenings, 7:00-8:30 p.m.

COLLEGE BOARD PREP COURSE **$25.00**
A class to prepare students to take the SAT exam. Provides an understanding of the skills being tested and emphasizes the development of reading comprehension and verbal proficiency. At the conclusion, students will take a typical exam, followed by a review of it. Six weeks. Wednesday class taught by Frank Finsthwait, teacher at The Westminster Schools. Students should bring **Barron's S.A.T. Review** *to first class. Wednesdays, 7:30-9:30 p.m. or Thursdays, 7:30-9:30 p.m.*

Arts, Crafts & Hobbies

WILLIAMSBURG FLOWER ARRANGING **$17.50**
Flower arrangements from plants and other materials found in your backyard and garden, as well as fields and woods. Taught by Mary Cooper. Six weeks. Thursday mornings, 9:30-10:55 a.m. or Thursday evenings, 7:30-8:55 p.m.

MICROWAVE CUISINE **$35.00**
All facets of microwave cooking: appetizers, eggs, meats, vegetables, desserts. Sample finished products. Taught by Ellen Buckley. Six weeks. Wednesday mornings, 10:00-11:30 a.m. or Tuesday evenings, 7:00-8:30 p.m.

BRIDGE **$20.00**
Taught by Fred Strickland, A.C.B.L. Life Master. Beginner course for those who have never played. Monday mornings, 9:00-10:25 a.m. or Tuesday evenings, 7:00-8:25 p.m.
Intermediate I for those who play but want to play better. Monday mornings, 10:30-11:55 or Tuesday afternoons, 1:30-2:55 or Tuesday evenings, 8:30-9:55 p.m.
Intermediate II for those who have taken an Intermediate course. Tuesday mornings, 10:30-11:55 a.m. or Monday evenings, 7:00-8:25 p.m.

FAMILY TREE **$22.50**
A genealogical do-it-yourself course covering major sources for basic family research in records, books and institutions. In and out-of-state research techniques and how to record data. Taught by Mae Ruth Green, professional genealogist. Tuesday evenings, 7:30-8:45 p.m. or Wednesday mornings, 10:00-11:15 a.m.

CERAMICS **$22.50**
Make beautiful decorations, gifts, and accessories for your home. Taught by LaVerne Rainer. Monday mornings, 9:30-11:30 a.m. or Tuesday evenings, 7:30-9:30 p.m.

CALLIGRAPHY **$17.50**
Learn to letter your invitations, place cards, greeting cards and name tags in the elegant old Italic hand. Taught by Kay Rogers and Carol Cumbie. Materials $10.00 (to be paid at first class). Wednesday mornings, 9:30-11:00 a.m. or Tuesday evenings, 7:30-9:00 p.m.

GUITAR **$25.00**
Learn to play popular songs by such artists as John Denver and Kenny Rogers. Taught by Charles Oliver. Tuesday evenings. Beginner, 6:30 p.m.; Beginner, 7:30 p.m.; Intermediate, 8:30 p.m.

HOME DECORATING **$15.00**
Course deals with color schemes, contrast level, furniture styles, making the most of accessories. Six weeks. Taught by Jansen Green Ford. Tuesday mornings, 9:30-10:30 a.m. or Thursday mornings, 9:30-10:30 a.m.

QUILTING **$22.50**
Create a memory for your family. Sew by hand or machine and use those remnants you have in the closet. Patterns include: Dresden Plate, Log Cabin, Bow Tie, Flying Geese, Crazy Quilt, Dutch Doll and many more. 4 weeks. Taught by Joanne Denise. Monday mornings, 10:00-12:00 noon.

Youth

"BE A SPORT"

A program to develop the pre-athletic skills young children will need to participate in various sports, such as football, soccer, basketball and baseball. Running, jumping, tumbling, dodging, kicking, throwing, catching, striking. Taught by Tim Straus, college and semi-pro athlete. **$15.00** *For 4 & 5 year olds - one afternoon a week.*

Tuesday afternoons, 3:30-4:15 p.m.
Wednesday afternoons, 3:30-4:15 p.m.
Thursday afternoons, 3:30-4:15 p.m.

Dance

BALLET FOR ADULTS $17.50
Improve posture and tone muscles. Taught by Bess Finch. Thursday mornings, 9:30-10:30 a.m. or Thursday evenings, 6:15-7:15 p.m. (Beginner), or 7:20-8:20 p.m. (for previous students).

MODERN JAZZ $17.50
A style of dance that promotes suppleness and coordination. Taught by Bess Finch. Thursday mornings, 10:30-11:30 a.m. or Thursday evenings, 8:25-9:25 p.m.

CHILDREN'S BALLET $17.50
An introduction to dance geared to the age of the child. Taught by Bess Finch. Ages 4-6. Thursday afternoons, 2:30-3:30 p.m. 2nd Year: Thursday afternoons, 3:30-4:30 p.m. Older children: Thursday afternoons, 4:30-5:30 p.m.

Sports

SOFTBALL
for Men and Women

We're going to be playing softball at Peachtree Presbyterian this spring, and you're invited to play with us. We'll have a league for men and one for women. The men's league is open to men and high school boys 16 and older; the women's league is open to women and high school girls 15 and older. Practices and games will be held at Garden Hills School field in the Buckhead area, and games will be played on weeknights during April, May and June.
Teams are limited to not more than 15 players so that everyone gets to play.
Our church members are given priority in registering, after which the program is open to persons in the community on a first-come-first-serve basis.

We'll send you complete information if you'll check the appropriate space on the application form and return to us.

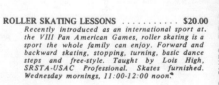

ROLLER SKATING LESSONS $20.00
Recently introduced as an international sport at the VIII Pan American Games, roller skating is a sport the whole family can enjoy. Forward and backward skating, stopping, turning, basic dance steps and free-style. Taught by Lois High, SRSTA-USAC Professional. Skates furnished. Wednesday mornings, 11:00-12:00 noon.

P.L.A.Y.

P.L.A.Y. stands for Planned Leisure Activities for Youngsters. It's Peachtree's unique summer recreation experience for boys and girls 6 to 11 years of age.
In P.L.A.Y. children do things that are fun. They make fishing poles and go fishing. They make toys in the Toy Workshop. They sing and laugh and play games and learn about God.
For complete information, check the appropriate space on the application form.

Boy Scouts

TROOP NO. 34 meets every Monday evening at 7:30 in our Family Center. Boys 11 to 15 years of age interested in outdoor activities, including hiking, camping and canoeing, should contact Scoutmaster Med Walstad at 255-4476.

In addition to participating in our Recreation Ministry, we call your attention to our . . .

Worship

SUNDAY MORNINGS: *8:30 and 11:00 a.m. Dr. W. Frank Harrington and our other ministers lead us in worship through meditation, sharing, illumination and service.*
"You enter this church, not as a stranger, but as a guest of Jesus Christ. Come, then, with joy in your heart and thanks on your lips, offering Him your love and service."
If you are unable to attend, we invite you to watch our service each Sunday evening at 7:00 p.m. on WHAE-Television, Channel 46.

Study

SUNDAY SCHOOL CLASSES: *Twelve different classes for adults offering a variety of subjects for men, women, couples and singles. We also offer classes for children of all ages. Sunday mornings at 9:30 a.m.*

Participation

THE PEACHTREE CONNECTION *happens on Wednesdays from mid-September through mid-May. You are invited to participate in all or any part:*

YOUTH CLUB: Our Christian education program featuring Bible study, music and recreation for boys and girls in the 1st through 7th grades. 4:15-6:30 p.m.

SUPPER: Served from 6:15 until 7:00 p.m.

BETHEL BIBLE SERIES: A two-year overview of the entire Bible. Meets from 7:30 until 8:30 p.m.

H.E.L.P. A variety of classes to "Help Equip Lay Persons" for Christian service. Includes in-depth Bible study, Christian beliefs, issues in Christian living, "how-to" minister to others.

Affiliation

PEACHTREE PRESBYTERIAN CHURCH *extends an invitation to you to join by (1) Profession of faith in Jesus Christ as the Son of God and Savior of sinners; (2) Re-affirmation of your faith if you are not now active in a Christian church; or (3) Transfer of your letter from another Christian church.*

One of our ministers would be delighted to talk with you about these and other opportunities at Peachtree. Call 261-7651 and let us share our Christian experience with you.

PEACHTREE PRESBYTERIAN CHURCH
3434 Roswell Road, N.W. • Atlanta, Georgia 30305
261-7651

...for the renewing of the spirit and making good the hurt. Winter '80

How to register

Classes and activities will begin the week of January 14th unless otherwise indicated. Classes meet for 8 weeks unless otherwise noted.

It is necessary to register in advance for all classes, and that you do so early, as enrollment is limited. You may register in person or by mail using the form below. Once you have registered, you will not be contacted prior to beginning of the class, so make a note of the starting day.

All classes will be held in the Family Center unless otherwise stated. A schedule showing the room in which your class meets will be posted on the bulletin board in the lower lobby.

Only if you withdraw from a class prior to its first meeting will your fees be refunded.

If you have any questions, please call us at 261-7651.

A nursery for children from 2 months to 4 years is provided during most morning classes. The fee (50¢ for the first hour and a half, $1.00 if longer) is payable when you bring your child.

Advanced registration, using the form below, is necessary.

RECREATION AT PEACHTREE

Class (or Activity)	Day(s)	Time	Fee
Participant's Name		Age (if child)	
Address		Home Phone	
City	Zip	Office Phone	
Parent's Name if Class is for Child		Please send information on:	
Church Affiliation		☐ Softball	
Nursery needed for		☐ P.L.A.Y.	
Name	Age		

Please return this form along with your check to:
Recreation Ministry, Peachtree Presbyterian Church
3434 Roswell Road, N.W., Atlanta, Georgia 30305
Telephone 261-7651

---

her husband goes through the mail, he too may linger on your brochure. "Photography" or "Guitar Lessons" may look interesting.

But whatever the case, now is the time for dealing with the facts: the "what," "when," "where," "how much" bit. It is at this point that the information needs to be both accurate and informative. It needs to be accurate so that the would-be participant knows what to expect from the activity.

In our D.I.E.T. (Diet Information & Exercise Training) class, we state:

> There are only two ways to lose weight: diet and exercise. This class combines both in a sensible approach to reaching and maintaining your desired weight.

The information is clear, concise, and truthful. It makes no promises of a "slimmer you," or that you'll be able to fit into last year's bathing suit. It, instead, approaches the problem of weight loss honestly and rationally.

The following information should be included about each class and activity:

> Name of class
> Brief description
> Cost
> Days and times it will be held
> Number of times it will meet
> Instructor's name (and biographical information, if appropriate)
> Materials students may need (if appropriate)

The following example from our brochure will illustrate this:

> COLLEGE BOARD PREP COURSE $25.00
> A class to prepare high school students to take the S.A.T. exam. Provides an understanding of the skills being tested and emphasizes the development of reading comprehension and verbal proficiency. At the conclusion, students will take a typical exam, followed by a review of it. Six weeks. Wednesday evenings, 7:30-9:30 P.M. Taught by Frank Finsthwait, teacher at The Westminster Schools. Students should bring *Barron's S.A.T. Review* to first class.

By reviewing the sample brochure (Winter '80) you can see how we've presented the facts in regard to a variety of classes and activities. As far as the description of the class goes, I request that the instructor of the class write a paragraph on the content of the class, which I then edit for publicity purposes. See also the "Softball at Peachtree" flyer which further illustrates how facts are presented in an orderly manner.

4. MAKE IT POSSIBLE TO RESPOND

Once the facts have been presented, give people a way to respond. They may be asked to call for further details; they may be instructed to come by to register; they may be requested to fill out a form and mail it in. In any case, give them a way to respond immediately, while the idea is fresh on their minds.

One of the best ways for them to respond is to have them fill out an application form and bring or mail it to you. Notice the sample application form printed at bottom of brochure. It asks for the usual information: the *class* for which they are registering, the *day(s)* it meets, the *time,* and the *fee.*

Information about the registrant is also requested: *name, address,* home and office *phone numbers.* Phone numbers are particularly useful so that we can call the registrant if a class is cancelled, or changed to a different time. We occasionally have persons come to the first class only to discover that it has been cancelled at the last moment and we were unable to contact them because they failed to list their phone numbers. This application form also has a place for the *parent's name* if the registrant is a child. Note that we also provide a space for a parent to register a child for the *nursery.* In addition, we ask for *church affiliation* so we can contact persons regarding our church if they are not members of another local church.

Sometimes it is not possible in a brochure that contains information on a variety of programs to give all the information needed about a particular activity. Our softball program is an example. Therefore, we *mention* the fact that the church has softball leagues for adults in the brochure that blankets the community, requesting that persons interested in receiving detailed information about softball place a check in the appropriate box on the application form. We then send them the complete information.

Preparing and Distributing Publicity

While all publicity should be directed at the right audience, be interesting, contain the necessary information, and provide a means of responding, there are a variety of ways to accomplish this. At one time or another, we employ all of the following: brochures, flyers, announcements in the church bulletin, personal announcements, radio spots, and newspaper announcements. Let's look at each of these as to production, cost, distribution, and what each accomplishes.

BROCHURES

One of the primary sources of our publicity is a quarterly brochure we call *Recreation at Peachtree.* It is our means of letting members of our church and the church community know about our recreation ministry in general. *Recreation at Peachtree* is a comprehensive promotional piece that lists all of the classes and activities that we offer in a given quarter. It is published each fall, winter, and spring.

Since it generally lists around thirty or so different activities, this brochure is not directed toward a specific audience, but rather is sent to the community in which our church serves. In addition to being sent to the home of each member, it is also sent to the residents living within a three-to-four mile radius of the church. We use a mailing service which sends the brochure to all homes and apartments in surrounding zip codes. The selection of zip codes is made by us based on the response to our program from each zip code in the past. Mailing services are listed in the Yellow Pages.

A brochure will give you the opportunity to present your program as a whole. Flyers and other announcements generally deal with specific activities in your overall program. I believe that a recreation ministry, regardless of size should publish a comprehensive brochure from the start. It need not be elaborate, but it will give your members and your community an overview of what you offer. Some churches publish a comprehensive brochure only one time a year, following up with supplements mailed out during the year. We don't do this since the original brochure is easily lost.

What should a brochure look like? Well, that's up to you. The brochure that we've pictured in this chapter was patterned after a menu that I saw at a local restaurant. We usually stick to a particular format for a year and then make a change. You will find it helpful to secure a number of brochures from other churches and use them to make comparisons so that you can decide on a format that appeals to you and will enable you to get your message across.

Bear in mind that a brochure is not inexpensive. The cost is determined by a number of factors, including: size, shape, typeface used, quality of paper, whether it is printed in more than one color, the printing process used, the number of folds it contains, and, of course, how many you have printed. A printer can advise you in these directions and also help in your decision as to design. Since printing is a highly competitive business, get several bids before choosing your printer.

In regard to layout, you'll notice that we present our program under several headings: Physical Fitness; Education; Arts, Crafts, & Hobbies; Youth; Dance; and Sports. The headings change from time to time, but

SOFTBALL AT PEACHTREE

Men and Women

NOW IS THE TIME TO REGISTER FOR SOFTBALL.

REGISTER EARLY TO ASSURE YOUR BEING PLACED ON A TEAM.

Leagues: Peachtree Presbyterian runs its own men's and women's leagues. We will have eight men's teams and four women's teams.

Field: All games will be played on the lighted Garden Hills School field, located in the Buckhead area on Sheridan Drive off Peachtree Road.

Schedule: Men's games on Monday and Thursday nights' women's on Tuesday—6:30 and 7:45 p.m. Teams will play once each week.

Season: Practice begins in mid-April; season runs from early May through June; tournaments—mid-July.

College Students: We will place out-of-town students (who are members of Peachtree) on teams when they return home, provided they register and pay fee now.

Ages: Open to men 15 years and older and women 15 and older, regardless of ability. No one is too old.

Evaluation: All players (except those who played at Peachtree last year) must be evaluated. Evaluation will take place at Garden Hills School field. Evaluation will be held on Saturday, April 12 —men at 11:00 a.m.; women at 12:00 noon. (Alternate evaluation date for both men and women: Monday, April 14, 6:00 p.m.) YOU MUST ATTEND THE EVALUATION IN ORDER TO PLAY. Teams will be organized to distribute ability as evenly as possible.

FEE: *$22.50 (numbered softball jersey included)*

- -

SOFTBALL AT PEACHTREE PRESBYTERIAN
3434 Roswell Road, N.W.
Atlanta, GA 30305   (261-7651)

NAME_____ Men_____ Women_____

ADDRESS_____ CITY_____

ZIP_____ HOME PHONE_____ OFFICE PHONE_____

Out-of-town college student_____ Will return home on_____

I played at Peachtree last year?   Yes_____ No_____ (If "No," check below)

I will attend evaluation on April 12_____ April 14_____

Amount enclosed $_____ I UNDERSTAND THAT THE FEE MUST ACCOMPANY
THIS REGISTRATION.

THE NUMBER OF TEAMS AND THE
PARTICIPANTS ON EACH TEAM IS
LIMITED. PLEASE REGISTER EARLY.

SIGNED_____

some kind of grouping gives a sense of order to the whole. As a matter of personal preference, I like to see everything presented in a brochure that opens up into a large format rather than in a number of pages that you have to turn through.

Note that on the back of the brochure we mention the total ministry of the church. Because this brochure reaches the hands of many unchurched and unsaved in the community, we extend an invitation to all to participate in our worship, study, and other church activities, and to consider uniting with us by profession of faith, reaffirmation, or transfer from another church.

FLYERS

Whereas our brochure is comprehensive in nature, most flyers published by our recreation ministry publicize special activities which will be of interest to a limited audience. Examples include: softball, basketball,

P.L.A.Y., etc. Flyers are generally produced by "quick-copy" or they may be mimeographed.

"Quick-copy" is an inexpensive process that has several advantages over mimeograph. While the printing is often done directly from your typewritten copy, "quick-copy" offers flexibility in using "clip art" and other pictures, can be done in different colored inks, and it produces clean, clear copies. Mimeograph, on the other hand, permits you to produce your own copies at minimum cost, and when the stencil is prepared by someone who is artistically inclined and familiar with the process, attractive flyers can be turned out on the spot.

Distribution of flyers is usually made by handing them out in Sunday school classes, leaving them at schools to be given out by teachers, mailing them to persons who have requested information on that activity, and mailing them to persons who have participated in

---

ADULT SUMMER RECREATION ACTIVITIES

Adult Ballet
Tues.— 9:15 a.m.   7:00 p.m.

Modern Jazz
Tues.—10:20 a.m.   8:05 p.m.
Fee $14.00—6 weeks

Ladies' Exercises
Morning: Mon., Wed. and Fri., 9:00 or 9:50 a.m. Fee: $22.50—8 weeks beginning June 11.
Evening: Mon. and Thurs., 6:00 or 7:00 p.m. Fee: $17.50—8 weeks beginning June 11.

Yoga Exercises
Morning: Thursday, 10:00 a.m.
Evening: Monday, 7:00 p.m.
Fee: $15.00—8 weeks, starts week of June 11.

Bridge
Beginner: Mon., 9:30 a.m., or Tues., 7:00 p.m.
Inter: Mon., 11:00 a.m. or Tues., 8:25 p.m.
Adv.: Tues. 10:30 a.m. or Mon. 7:00 p.m.
Fee: $17.50—8 weeks beginning June 11.

Activity _____
Date begins _____ Time _____
Name _____
Address _____
City _____ Zip _____
Home ph _____ Office ph _____
Amt. paid _____

Please return to: Recreation, Peachtree Presbyterian Church, 3434 Roswell Road, N.W., Atlanta, Ga. 30305. Phone 261-7651.

P.L.A.Y.
P.L.A.Y. stands for Planned Leisure Activities for Youngsters. It's Peachtree's unique summer recreation experience for boys and girls 6 to 10 years of age.
In P.L.A.Y. children do things that are fun. They make their own fishing poles and actually go fishing in a pond stocked with bream. They make toys in the Toy Workshop. They sing, and laugh, and play games, and learn about God.
P.L.A.Y. is directed by Tim Straus and Allison Smith, both college students and members of Peachtree.
Each session of P.L.A.Y. will last for one week, from 9:00 A.M. to 3:30 P.M.
6 & 7 years—June 11-15, 25-29, July 16-20
8-10 years—June 18-22, July 9-13
Fee: $25.00 per week. A $10 deposit will reserve a place.

Activity _____

Date Begins _____ Time _____

Name of Child _____

Age _____

Parent's Name _____

Address _____

City _____ Zip _____

Office Phone _____ Home Phone _____
$_____
Amount Paid

Please return to: Recreation, Peachtree Presbyterian Church, 3434 Roswell Road, N.W., Atlanta, Ga. 30305. Phone 261-7651.

BASKETBALL CAMP (August 6 - 10) FOR: Boys 7 & 8; Girls 8 - 10

MORNINGS: Basic ball-handling skills such as: dribbling, passing, shooting, rebounding.

AFTER LUNCH: Quiet time for game strategy using movies and chalk-talks.

MID-AFTERNOON: Will cover offensive moves, playmaking, man-to-man and zone defense.

TO CLOSE OUT DAY: Scrimmage.

BASKETBALL GOALS: Will be set at a height appropriate to child's age.

DIRECTED BY: Bobby Ward, junior varsity basketball coach at Westminster School.
STAFF: Players from Westminster teams.

TIME CAMP MEETS: 9 A.M. - 4 P.M.

Activity _____ Date Begins _____

Name _____

Age _____ Time _____

Parent's Name _____

Address _____

_____ Zip _____

Home Phone _____ Office Phone _____
PLEASE RETURN TO:

Recreation
Peachtree Presbyterian Church
3434 Roswell Road, N.W.
Atlanta, GA 30305
Phone: 261-7651

similar activities in the past, e.g., if someone played in our softball league last year, we will be sure that person gets a flyer on it again.

ANNOUNCEMENTS

The weekly church bulletin provides a quick way of notifying your members about programs and activities that will affect them. It will probably represent your most used form of publicity. And don't forget the opportunity it affords to provide an on-going "education" of the membership in regard to recreation. If recreation is to be an integral part of the total ministry of the church, you must keep it before the congregation. I believe that few weeks should go by in which some mention of the recreation ministry is not made. And this kind of publicity does not always have to be "selling." It will be one of your best ways of "reporting" on things that have taken place: golf tourney winners, softball standings,

volunteers who have served, etc. I've included several examples of items from our past bulletins.

Don't overlook the possibilities for making personal announcements before Sunday school classes, at fellowship dinners, and from the pulpit. Some of the most successful programs we've had in our church have been the ones that were verbally promoted at various gatherings. When you've got a program you're excited about, there's no beter way to promote it than by telling someone first-hand. You'll also have a chance to get feedback and answer questions that would not have been asked unless you were there. And few, if any, can make a better "pitch" than one who's talking about his or her own program. The next best thing to do is have members of your recreation committee each take one Sunday school class, preferably the one to which they belong, and make verbal announcements at times when they are needed for promotion.

INTRAMURAL VOLLEYBALL LEAGUES

Men's and women's "in-house" volleyball leagues will be organized on *Monday, September 17, at 8:30 P.M.*: games will be played on the following six Monday nights. AAU rules will govern play. *ALL* players *MUST* attend the evaluation on September 17 at 8:30 P.M. Register and pay in advance to assure a spot on a team, as enrollment is limited. Fee: $7.50.

Name_____

Address_____Zip_____

Men_____Women_____Amt. Pd._____

Home Phone_____Office Phone_____

RECREATION

SOFTBALL STANDINGS—Peachtree had 8 men's and 4 women's teams in its intramural softball league this summer.

The men's team, coached by Henry Green (record 6 wins—1 loss), and the women's team, coached by Greg Bourne (6-1), were the season's winners. Post-season tournament champions were Tom Sellers' men's team and the women's team coached by Bill Maness.

HOLIDAY OPEN GYM PERIODS

The gym will be open the following
times during the holidays:

Monday, December 18, 6:00-9:30 P.M.
Tuesday, December 19, 6:00-9:30 P.M.
Wednesday, December 27, 6:00-9:30 P.M.
Thursday, December 28, 6:00-9:30 P.M.

Recreation News

HUNTING TIPS

Tips on hunting: game habitats, methods of hunting, use of dogs, with emphasis on careful observance of both the laws of man and nature. Presented by John Martin, whose "Inside Outdoors" has been in newspapers and on radio and television for 31 years.

Tuesday evenings, 7:30-9:30 P.M., beginning October 3rd.
Fee: $10.00—4 weeks.

Please enroll me in Hunting Tips. Enclosed is a check for $10.00.

Name_____ Phone_____

GOLF TOURNAMENT

Our fall golf tournament, open to all Peachtree members (men, women, boys and girls) and their guests, will be played on Monday, October 2nd at Tam-O-Shanter Country Club in Roswell.

Each foursome will consist of an A, B, C & D player (based on estimated score given below) and we will use the Ft. Lauderdale system of play.

Tee-off time will be 1:00 P.M. The fee will be $14.00 (cart included).

Please sign me up for the fall golf tournament.

Name_____ Est. Score_____

Address_____

Zip_____ Home Phone_____ Office Phone_____

GOLF WINNERS

Our fall golf tournament was won by the team of Al McGhee, Alan Boyles, Katy Smith, and Bob Chambless. Playing under the Ft. Lauderdale system, they shot an eight-under, 63. The longest drive by a man and woman were made by Dan Hicks and Bonnie Kempton, and Roy Torbert came closest to the pin.

Foursomes were determined by a draw so that no one knew who he would be playing with until tee-off time. Consequently, everyone was a winner in that many new friendships were begun.

PEACHTREE COLLEGE VOLLEYBALL TOURNAMENT

On Wednesday and Thursday evenings, December 20th and 21st, our church will host the first Peachtree Invitational Christmas Men's Volleyball Tournament. We have extended an invitation to four other churches in our area to submit one team each, and would hope that our church would enter *two* teams. We will play in round-robin fashion over the two-day period so no teams will be eliminated. Winners will be determined by total number of points scored for all games played. Play will begin each evening at 7:00 P.M. Open to any young man of college age. See either Bill Scurry or John Spencer to register.

RADIO SPOTS

Radio stations are mandated by law to provide a certain amount of air time to public service announcements. This is a good source of free publicity. However, stations are bombarded with requests for such and must, therefore, be selective in choosing the ones that are broadcast. To be sure yours gets aired, keep it short and to the point. A public service announcement is no place to be "cute." Leave that for the professionals who are paying for the time.

Here's an example of an announcement that ran on four stations for one week, and we had to turn people away at the door:

> Want to play volleyball? Peachtree Presbyterian Church invites individuals to register for its men's and women's intramural volleyball leagues. Teams will be organized on Monday evening, September 17th, at 7:30 P.M. For more information, call 261-7651.

Check with the radio stations in your area to find out how they want the information presented to them. Some prefer it on 3" x 5" cards which they date and drop in a file box to be read as they come up. The easier you make it for the station, the more likely you are to get your announcement on the air. Another thing, know your station's audience. Some play rock music, some popular, some classical, some are all news. Don't send what you want teenagers to hear to a classical or all news station.

NEWSPAPER ANNOUNCEMENTS

Some newspapers, particularly suburban dailies and weeklies, will be interested in features on activities presently taking place. They are generally interested, however, in *reporting* current activities and not *promoting* future ones, but a feature story on your ongoing activities will be helpful for the next series of classes. Your best bet is to see if your newspaper has a "leisure" section in which they regularly run announcements on community activities — concerts, tours, lectures, recreation opportunities, etc. People often scan this section "looking for something" in the area of recreation. Again, this is no place to be "cute." Make it straightforward and concise. Check with the papers to find out their requirements.

Here's an example of one that was successful for us:

> Peachtree Presbyterian Church, 3434 Roswell Road, N.W. offers "Be a Sport" for 4-6-year-olds to develop pre-athletic skills for football, soccer, basketball, and baseball. Afternoon classes on Tuesday and Thursday. Fee: $15.00 for eight weeks. Call 261-7651.

As I pointed out earlier, publicity is the key to your success. I frequently "overkill" with publicity because I don't think you can have too much. In most cases, I publicize in every way I've mentioned above for nearly every major activity.

When Should Publicity "Go Out"?

The answer to that question is that it should go out in time for recipients to make the necessary arrangements to participate (line up a babysitter, schedule around other activities, arrange a car-pool, etc.), and yet not so early that they put off signing up and then forget.

Parents will need to know a month or so ahead of time in order to schedule children's sports activities around music lessons, Boy Scouts, Brownies, and various other activities. Summer activities, such as day camps, should be publicized even earlier so that they can be scheduled around vacations. Adult classes, on the other hand, should, we have found, be publicized about two or three weeks ahead of time.

We follow a policy of notifying our own members before we send any publicity out to the community at large. That way, members have ample opportunity to register before classes fill.

On Distributing Information in Schools

I make it a point to meet the principals of all schools in my church's area. I tell them about the kinds of programs we offer for children, how everyone is welcome — regardless of race or religion, how everyone participates — regardless of ability. I suggest that I would like to, from time to time, bring by information to be distributed to the students. I tell them that my flyers will be counted and bundled and ready to be placed in the teacher's mailboxes, so they can distribute them to their classes. I have found that most principals are quite responsive to this approach to publicity, if they are convinced that the program you offer will be of benefit to their students.

If you plan to do this, be sure to ascertain how many different classes are involved and what is the largest number of students in any one class. Then, when you bring your flyers to the school, have them bundled, with each bundle containing enough for the largest class. You can wear out your welcome if you overdo this. I do not distribute information in schools more than two or three times a year.

5

FINANCING:
Paying for Your Program

Recreation costs money. Teachers have to be hired. Equipment has to be purchased. Uniforms have to be bought. Publicity has to be paid for. How will you finance your recreation ministry?

You may choose to underwrite the cost of your recreation ministry out of the church budget, allocating funds to cover the anticipated expenses. On the other hand, you may decide to operate your ministry of recreation on a self-supporting basis — where the ministry itself will generate sufficient income to offset its costs.

The choice of how to finance your recreation ministry needs to be made early in your planning so that you can establish some guidelines for budgeting for your programs. In this chapter, we'll look at some advantages and disadvantages of each, make a recommendation based on our experience, and then outline some practical steps for the preparation of a recreation budget.

Allocation vs. Self-Supporting

Many churches have opted to include recreation in the overall budget of the church. Money is thereby allocated to salaries, equipment, publicity, etc. When this is the case, members are usually asked to increase their pledges to cover the expenses of this additional ministry. In some instances, a separate gift to the recreation ministry is requested over and above the pledge to the church. Such an approach to financing obviously encourages a sense of stewardship among members for the recreation ministry.

On the other hand, a recreation ministry, if it is significant, can place a strain on a church's budget, and perhaps, even more so, siphon off money that otherwise would be designated for benevolent giving. Some churches have elected, therefore, to set up the financing of their recreation ministry on a self-supporting basis whereby expenses incurred are offset by fees charged to participants. While it is true that members will then have to "pay" to participate in certain aspects of their recreation ministry, most will heartily endorse a self-supporting recreation ministry in light of the obvious advantages.

First of all, there is no drain on the treasury of tithes and offerings. Benevolent projects need not be curtailed. Secondly, the *growth* of the ministry is not limited to the funds that have been allocated. Under the former, you would have to turn people away, for example, if you had alloted only enough money to equip and sponsor one men's softball team, and you had enough sign up for three teams. Thirdly, by operating on a self-supporting basis, the freedom to add new programs at any time would not be lessened by the unavailability of funds. Rather, you would simply determine a fee that would cover the costs of the new program. Fourthly, and perhaps most important of all, when each participant pays for the cost of a program, non-members can participate at no additional financial burden to the church. In fact, non-member participation will often give you the additional persons needed to fill your classes. And, in addition, having non-member participation will enable you, through your recreation ministry, to bring many unchurched and unsaved persons into your church and in contact with your members and the coaches and/or other leaders whom you have recruited.

We have found that a position somewhere in between has worked well for us. Indirect expenses are allocated from the church budget. They include: the minister's or director's salary, building maintenance costs (including janitorial help, cleaning supplies, repair and replacement of original building equipment), and utilities. Direct expenses — those relating to programming — are covered by program fees. They include: salaries for a secretary, part-time help, teachers, sports' officials; league fees; equipment (including everything from basketballs and softball bats to rollerskates to record players and movie projectors to ping-pong tables and tumbling mats); publicity; postage; stationary; etc.

In other words, if we were going to run a men's basketball league in our gym, the cost of the gym itself, as well as the cost of heating, lighting, and maintaining it, would be borne by the church budget. On the other hand, the cost of balls, officials, uniforms, publicity, and a pro-rated portion of the secretary's salary would come from fees.

Note that when just starting a recreation ministry, some costs may have to be absorbed by the church budget until the programs become established to the point that they generate sufficient revenue. By charging fees to cover the costs of programming, a church can maintain a recreation ministry without compromising on the other financial commitments it has, and, at the same time, have the flexibility needed for growth and creativity in programming.

Determining Fees

Assuming that you are going to charge fees to cover the costs of your classes and activities, how do you determine how much that will be? How much will you charge for an exercise class, for example? How much to play softball?

NON-SPORTS FEES

Setting fees is a matter of determining the costs involved in a particular class or activity; estimating the number of participants that can be expected to enroll; and then dividing the number of participants into the cost.

For instance, let's say that you want to offer an exercise class for women. You agree to pay an instructor $20 per day, two days a week, for a period of eight weeks. Her salary would be $20 × 2 days × 8 weeks = $320.00. Assuming that she would provide her own music (record player and records), that the class would be held in a carpeted room (so no exercise mats would be needed), and that you would promote the class in your church's weekly bulletin (at no additional cost to your budget), the total cost of the class would be the instructor's salary.

Now, let's say that you can reasonably expect 20 women to register for the class. By dividing the cost ($320) by the number of participants (20), you would have a fee of $16.00. You may choose to set a fee of $17.50 or even $20 to cover any contingencies. This procedure can be followed for each class or activity.

As your program grows, however, there will be additional expenses, over and above the instructor's salary. If you want to reach non-church-members, you will have to publicize. Printing and mailing brochures is costly. And when people read about your program, they will want to find out more about it, and they will call or come by the church. Additional phone lines will have to be installed, and someone will have to answer the phone and talk to those who come by. You will be able to get by with a volunteer at first, but eventually, you will have to hire a secretary. She will need an office with a typewriter, a calculator, file cabinets, and supplies, all of which costs money.

If you have a recreation facility, someone will have to be on duty whenever programs are going on. That probably means part-time help during the afternoon and evening hours, and that adds to the payroll. And, there will be equipment to purchase and repair and replace: basketballs, rollerskates, ping-pong tables, card tables, movie projectors, phonographs, tumbling mats, and so on. How much will all of these things cost?

Figuring these additional expenses is precarious at best. Some costs increase in proportion to the program. The more programming you do, the more hours you will need a secretary. The more hours your building is open, the more supervisory personnel you'll need. The more classes and activities you schedule, the more publicity you'll have to prepare and distribute.

On the other hand, there'll be some items of equipment that you will have to purchase in order to begin certain classes (tumbling mats for a tumbling class, for instance). Once they have been bought, however, they will be used over and over again as the class is repeated.

Is there a way to determine fees that takes all of these and other additional expenses into consideration? I have found through trial-and-error, that, as a rule of thumb, it takes about 40% of the total income produced by fees from classes and activities to cover the additional expenses of a recreation ministry where a recreation facility is involved. That is to say, when all of the additional expenses are averaged out over several years, about 40% of the income from classes and activities is needed to cover these expenses. Therefore, I have found that the formula presented in chapter 3 on Staff has provided a workable method of determining fees for our programs, which over the long run will enable our ministry to operate on a break-even basis.

The formula, as you will recall, is:

$$\frac{}{\text{Rate}} \times \frac{}{\substack{\text{\# of}\\\text{Classes}}} = \frac{\$}{\text{Salary}} \div .6 = \frac{\$}{\substack{\text{Income}\\\text{Needed}}} \div \frac{}{\substack{\text{Minimum Fee}\\\text{Enrollment}}} = \frac{\$}{}$$

Note that the formula uses a factor of 0.6. By dividing the salary by 60% (0.6) you will determine the *income needed* in order to pay the salary and still have 40% remaining to cover the additional expenses. I use the formula for determining the fee that we will charge for all Arts, Crafts, and Hobbies; Fitness; and Youth classes. (For sports, I use a different method, which is outlined below.)

If you do not have a recreation facility *per se,* your additional expenses will be less, and you may not need 40% to cover these. Thirty percent or even 20% may suffice, in which case, you simply divide by 0.7 or 0.8 respectively.

SPORTS FEES

In determining the fees for sports programs, I simply estimate the costs, add 10% for contingencies, and divide by the anticipated number of participants.

Let's look at two examples which will illustrate this:

Determining Fees for a Softball Team

Let's assume that you want to enter a softball team in a church league. Assume that the league fee is $175 per team, that you will furnish jerseys for your players (that they will keep after the season is over), as well as bats and sufficient balls for practice, and that your team will have no more than fifteen players.

The cost of fielding a team would be:
League fee	$175.00
Softball jerseys (15 @ $5.00)	75.00
Bats (3 @ $15.00)	45.00
Balls (6 @ $5.00)	30.00
COST	$325.00
10% for contingencies	32.00
TOTAL	$357.00

When you divide the total by the number of players (fifteen), the individual fee would be $24.00.

Determining Fees for a Softball League

Assume in this case that you have been able to secure a field for two nights a week (at $12 per night, to cover maintenance and lighting) and your church would like to conduct a league of its own and invite other churches in the community to enter teams. Suppose that you will limit the number of teams in the league to eight, that you will play a seven-game-season and conclude with a consolation tournament. The entire season and tournament would consist of twenty-eight regular games plus eleven tournament games for a total of thirty-nine. The cost of running such a league might look something like this:

Field expenses (12 weeks to allow for make-up games)	
12 weeks × 2 nights × $12.00	$288.00
Umpires (2 per game @ $7.50 each)	585.00
Balls (avg. of 1½ per game @ $5.00)	295.00
Publicity & promotion	100.00
COST	$1268.00
10% contingency	127.00
TOTAL	$1395.00

By dividing the total by eight teams, you would have a team fee of $175.00

Budgeting

Budgeting is simply a matter of combining the various elements of financing into a schedule of anticipated income and expense. Because we divide our recreation ministry into four program areas, we prepare our budget accordingly. The following is an example of how we assign amounts to the various elements:

INCOME
> Allocation (Money from church budget allocated for recreation)
> Program
>> Arts & Crafts (fees from arts & crafts classes)
>> Fitness (fees from fitness classes)
>> Youth (fees from youth classes and activities)
>> Sports (fees from sports activities)

EXPENSES
> Secretary (salary, FICA, and benefits)*
> Part-time Help (salaries and FICA)*
> Equipment and Supplies (not related to sports)*
> Publicity*
>> (*The total of these items should equal 40% of the income from Arts & Crafts, Fitness, and Youth.)
> Program
>> Arts & Crafts (salaries, equal to 60% of income)
>> Fitness (salaries, equal to 60% of income)
>> Youth (equal to 60% of income)
>> Sports (equal to 100% of income)

Now, let's put some numbers in the budget. Suppose, for the sake of space, we budget for one quarter. We'll use the spring quarter, since we've already prepared figures on softball. In the areas of Arts & Crafts, Fitness, and Youth, we have calculated the income needed from each class or activity using the formula with the factor of 0.6.

BUDGET

PROGRAM AREA	CLASS	SALARY	÷ .6 =	INCOME NEEDED
Arts & Crafts	Bridge (beg. — A.M.)	240		400
	Bridge (int. — A.M.)	240		400
	Bridge (beg. — P.M.)	300		500
	Bridge (int. — P.M.)	300		500
	Calligraphy	240		400
	Guitar	240		400
	Ballet — A.M.	360		600
	Ballet — P.M.	360		600
	Water Color	240		400
	Quilting	120		200
	Needlepoint	120		200
TOTAL (Arts & Crafts)		$2760		$4600
Fitness	Ladies' Exercise — A.M.	480		800
	Ladies' Exercise — P.M.	300		500
	Yoga — A.M.	240		400
	Yoga — P.M.	240		400
TOTAL (Fitness)		$1260		$2100
Youth	Fitniks	300		500
	Be-a-Sport	300		500
TOTAL (Youth)		$600		$1000

By using these figures, along with those calculated earlier for a softball league, the budget would look like this:

INCOME

    Allocation . . . .
    Program
        Arts & Crafts 4600.00
        Fitness 2100.00
        Youth 1000.00
        Sports 1400.00
    TOTAL INCOME $9100.00

EXPENSE

    Secretary 1200.00
    Part-time Help 600.00
    Equipment & Supplies 300.00
    Publicity 980.00
    Program
        Arts & Crafts 2760.00
        Fitness 1260.00
        Youth 600.00
        Sports 1400.00
    TOTAL EXPENSE $9100.00

The financing and budgeting procedures described in this chapter have worked well for us. You may want to employ them, perhaps with some modification to suit your situation, until you can develop a system of your own.

6

SPORTS:
Competitive Programming

As a child, I can remember spending many youth basketball games sitting on the bench. I don't remember whether we won or lost those games; I just remember that I kept the bench warm. Even as a teenager, I can remember "playing" church league basketball, most of the time, again, from the bench. As an adult, I have had more than my share of bench sitting in adult church league basketball games, getting into action only when it was obvious we had already won or lost the game.

Now, the interesting thing is that I'm not that bad an athlete. I played baseball throughout high school, in college, and have coached collegiate baseball. But, for one reason or another, I never had the opportunity to really play basketball, and, consequently, did not develop the rudiments of the game.

Since becoming recreation director at Peachtree, I have begun to acquire some degree of skill in basketball, at least to the extent that I feel comfortable on the court. This is due to the fact that when I became director, I instituted a policy that everyone would play a minimum of half of every game. Consequently, by playing regularly, I've picked up enough to know what to do with the ball. If I'd had that opportunity as a child, I might have turned out to be pretty good.

A Philosophy of Playing

In collegiate athletics, winning is important. Consequently, as a college baseball coach, I played the best players. In church athletics, there's something more important than winning. When I became recreation director, our church had a tradition of winning. We had acquired a number of trophies as our men's basketball and softball teams were usually in the inter-church league championships.

My concern was that I suspected that there were many persons in our church who might have wanted to play but knew they weren't good enough. So, with the endorsement of the recreation committee, we decided to organize our own men's basketball league and open it to anyone who wanted to play just for the fun of it. As a result, we not only had our "traveling" team, composed of the best athletes, we had to close out registration when we enrolled enough "others" for eight teams. Interestingly, the next season, the traveling team was abandoned for lack of interest as many of the players on that team had joined our new league because they found out that the rest of us were having such a good time.

Admittedly, it has taken a lot of encouraging among members to persuade them that they are welcome regardless of age or ability. But because of it, we have men and women playing basketball, softball, and volleyball who have not played (or thought of playing) competitive sports in years.

In one instance, I was organizing a women's basketball team and had asked each player to introduce herself and tell the last time she had played basketball. One lady sheepishly stated that the last time she played was her senior year in college in 1963. The young lady next to her laughed as she said that was the year she was born. But the teenager and the mother of two played together that year, and they have continued to do so ever since. In fact, we have several instances in which fathers and sons and mothers and daughters play on the same teams.

The second year of our women's basketball program

one lady, who could have passed for anybody's grand-mother lied about her age on the application form. She later told someone she was afraid she would be considered too old to play. In the last game of the season, she scored eight points in her team's four-point victory.

The point I am trying to make is that I believe that a church's athletic program should not be exclusively for the young and athletic. Youth or ability should not be a prerequisite to participation. This philosophy has been borne out by the response of the members of this church and the community. Ever since, we have operated at capacity in all of our sports programs where we have over seventy-five different teams competing annually. You ask, how can it work? How can highly skilled athletes and those not blessed with a lot of athletic ability compete together in a program that is mutually satisfying? The answer is in our system of evaluation and distribution of ability.

Evaluation and Distribution of Ability

Prior to playing in any of our athletic programs, we require that every man, woman, boy, and girl be evaluated to determine his or her athletic ability. This is not a demeaning experience, but rather one done in an atmosphere of fun and fellowship, with no pressure on any individual to perform well. In basketball, for instance, we watch each participant dribble, shoot jump shots, layups, and free throws. We rate their performance on a scale (Details for each evaluation are discussed in the section on "Team Sports."), and then rank the players according to our evaluation of their ability.

The evaluation is done by those persons who will be coaching in that particular sport. In our adult leagues, these coaches then draft players until all have been chosen. When we finish, every team is, at least as far as we can ascertain, equal to every other in ability. In our youth sports program, we follow a little different procedure. Instead of drafting, the coaches together divide the players into teams. When each coach is satisfied that all the teams are as even in ability as they can make them, they each select their team in a *blind* draw.

By having teams of equal ability as far as physical talent is concerned, and by requiring that everyone play a minimum of half of every game, we have found a system that not only accommodates varied levels of ability on the same team, it also has a unifying effect in building team spirit. As you can imagine, such a system works best *within* the church family. But, it will also work in competition between different churches, if the churches involved are willing to cooperate in establishing rules and policies that foster participation.

Intra-church vs. Inter-church Competition

Whenever possible, I am in favor of intra-church athletic competition, that is, competition among teams within your own church. In intra-church athletics, you and your committee can establish those rules and policies which best enable you to minister through athletic competition. More importantly, an intra-church athletic program will give you more opportunities to witness to your community through a recreation ministry that readily accommodates non-members. And, an intra-church athletic program is more feasible than you might think. (Details for intra-church competition will be discussed in the section on "Team Sports.)

On the other hand, there will be some sports programs and some age groups within sports programs in which you will want to enter into leagues with other churches. In these instances, it is important for recreation directors to work cooperatively in the establishment and implementation of goals which will make competitive athletics a ministry to all who participate.

A Ministry of Athletics

Before exploring the "how-tos" of sports programming, let me say something about the exciting possibilities for ministry that are inherent in church athletics. I believe, in fact, that it is through athletics that a recreation ministry can make its greatest impact for both Christian evangelism and nurture: evangelism, in that a sports program will, for many, be their first introduction to the life of the church; nurture, as the children of God through playing together express their joy in Christ and in one another. But evangelism and nurture will not occur by chance. If the primary concerns of your athletic program are competition and winning, instead of participation and fellowship, then little in the way of evangelism and nurture will occur.

If you believe that the purpose of recreation in the church is to be a ministry, it is incumbent upon you to see that that ministry is fulfilled. How do you do it? Through the *recruitment* and *training* of your coaches. I am convinced that most recreation directors do not give top priority to the recruiting and training of those persons who will most directly influence the actions and attitudes of the participants in their sports program. It is a fact that through your coaches, and what you instill in them, you will succeed or fail in making your athletic program a ministry. In that regard, your task is not unlike that of Jesus in the selection and preparation of his disciples who would ultimately carry on his ministry. We'll have a lot to say about the recruiting and training of coaches in the following sections.

Team Sports

In this section, we'll examine "Team Sports" from the standpoint of how-to organize and operate youth and adult basketball leagues and adult softball and volleyball leagues. These are the ones that you will generally find most popular in church recreation programs. The principles outlined herein will apply, however, to other team sports which your church may want to sponsor.

YOUTH BASKETBALL

In our youth basketball program, we stress fundamentals, participation, and sportsmanship: fundamentals, in that we want children to become better basketball players as a result of participating with us; participation, in that children not only play half of every game, they are also given equal opportunity to learn to play during practice, regardless of their ability; sportsmanship, in that we want children to discover that winning and losing are not necessarily reflected by the number of points on either side of the scoreboard.

Age Groups

As children's skill level, interest, and attention span are directly related to age, grouping according to age is important. We have found that children practice and play well together when there is only one year's difference in age. More spread than that makes it difficult for both the older and younger children on a team. Our groupings are as follows:

Boys 7 & 8 years
Boys 9 & 10 years
Boys 11 & 12 years
Boys 13 & 14 years (Jr. High)
Boys 15 and older* (High School)

*Boys 17 and older may choose to play in our adult leagues if they desire.

Girls 10 & under*
Girls 11 & 12
Girls 13 & 14
Girls 15 & older (play in our women's league)

*Eight-year-old girls are welcome in this age group as there are no 7-& 8-year-old girls' leagues in our community.

Age is determined as of September 1st, as that coincides with our school system's delineation.

We make certain modifications in regard to court dimensions, basket height, and ball size to accommodate our younger age groups. Those who have studied the development of basketball skills in young children have found that lowering the basket, shortening the shooting distance for free throws, playing on a smaller court, and reducing the size of the ball facilitate the learning process. Children learn to pass and shoot the ball more naturally when they don't have to *heave* in the direction they want it to go. Consequently, we make the following modifications:

Court size:	*Youth (38' × 66', or thereabout)*	
	7 & 8 Boys	
	9 & 10 Boys	
	10 & under Girls	
Basket height:	*8½ feet*	*9 feet*
	7 & 8 Boys	9 & 10 Boys
		10 & under Girls
Free throw line:	*9 feet*	*12 feet*
	7 & 8 Boys	9 & 10 Boys
		10 & under Girls
Basketball size:	*Junior*	
	7 & 8 Boys	
	10 & under Girls	

In addition, our officials are not as strict in calling fouls and violations with younger age groups. This will be discussed in detail in the section on "Training of Officials."

Evaluation Procedure

As pointed out earlier, we require all participants (even those who have played with us in previous years) to be evaluated prior to being assigned to a team. As this will be an introduction to our program for the new players, we regard this not as a chore to be gotten over, but as an opportunity to meet old friends who have played with us before and to greet newcomers and make them feel welcome. We don't rush through the evaluation, but rather try to make an enjoyable experience out of it for everyone involved. The evaluation is usually scheduled on the afternoon or evening when that age group will practice.

Parents often accompany their children to the evaluation, so we provide a place in the gym where they can sit and watch. At the same time, we use this as an opportunity to do a little public relations. In addition to introducing the coaches, talking briefly about our program and its philosophy, we give out a flyer on the evaluation procedure and what to expect next. A copy of our flyer is included.

See our publicity sheet, "Basketball at Peachtree," which contains the evaluation times so that players and their parents will be aware of the evaluation time when they register. Note on the publicity sheet that persons who, because of some conflict, cannot attend the regularly scheduled evaluation, are asked to call the recreation office for an alternate time. The alternate time is

EVALUATION PROCEDURE

We're delighted to have your child participating in our basketball program here at Peachtree.

Today the coaches in your child's league will evaluate all the children to see how well they can jump, shoot free throws and layups, and dribble.

We'll then tally the scores and divide the players into teams of equal ability. Once all of the coaches agree that the teams are as equal as we can make them, they will select a team in a blind draw.

Each coach will then call the children on his or her team and notify them as to the time for the first practice.

You will be interested to know that our coaches are required to attend coaches' clinics which we conduct each fall. In these workshops, we discuss rules and modifications that pertain to various age groups, planning practices, coaching responsibilities, as well as our philosophy of athletics for young people.

Practice schedules are as follows:

7&8 Boys	Mon. 4:30-5:45 p.m.	Sat. 9:00-10:15 a.m.
9&10 Boys	Tue. 4:30-5:45 p.m. Tue. 5:45-7:00 p.m.	Sat. 10:15-11:30 a.m. (4 teams) Sat. 11:30-12:45 p.m. (2 teams)
11&12 Boys	Thurs. 4:30-5:45 p.m.	Sat. 12:45-2:00 p.m.
13&14 Boys	Tue. 5:45-7:00 p.m.	Sat. 11:30-12:45 p.m.
15-17 Boys	Wed. 8:30-10:00 p.m.	To be scheduled
8-10 Girls	Mon. 5:45-7:00 p.m.	Sat. 2:00-3:15 p.m.
11&12 Girls	Mon. 5:45-7:00 p.m.	Sat. 2:00-3:15 p.m.

If you have any questions in regard to our program, please feel free to ask.

Bill Maness, Recreation
Mike Cavanagh, Basketball Director

```
┌─────────────────────────────────┐
│                                 │
│        EVALUATION CARD          │
│                                 │
│   26                            │
│   ──                            │
│   #                             │
│                                 │
│                                 │
│   TOMMY SMITH                   │
│   ─────────────────────────     │
│   NAME                          │
│                                 │
│   261 4082            10        │
│   ─────────────     ──────      │
│   PHONE               AGE       │
│                                 │
│                                 │
│   Jump  ( 74 " )      2         │
│                     ──────      │
│   Dribble             3+        │
│                     ──────      │
│   Free Throw          2         │
│                     ──────      │
│   Layup               3         │
│                     ──────      │
│                                 │
│   TOTAL SCORE         10        │
│                     ──────      │
│                                 │
└─────────────────────────────────┘
```

The skills tested are:

1. Jumping for height
2. Free throw shooting
3. Layup shooting
4. Dribbling

In *jumping for height,* each child jumps and marks with a piece of chalk on a ruled board attached to the gym wall the highest point he or she can reach. This takes into account not only jumping ability but height as well. After all jumps have been recorded, those who are in the top third of the jumpers are given a score of "3"; those in the middle third, "2"; those in the bottom third, "1." Any child with an outstanding jumping ability, regardless of the total height reached, is given a " + " by his or her score.

In *free throw shooting,* the coach looks for strength (ease with which the child makes the shot) and technique. In *layup shooting,* the comparison is based on technique and accuracy. In *dribbling* (through an obstacle course of chairs or other objects), ball handling ability with one or both hands is assessed.

To facilitate the evaluation process, an evaluation card (see sample) is filled out beforehand with the child's name, age, phone number, and a number which corresponds to a number on an accompanying sheet of paper which is pinned onto the child's shirt for identification purposes. The children are then divided into four groups and rotate from one station to another.

Before they leave, we bring them back together to once again welcome them to our program and to answer any questions they may have. At that time they are told to expect a call from their coach in a few days.

When the evaluation is completed, the coaches meet together to add the scores of the four skills to determine each child's total score. The coaches then begin the process of distributing the ability of the various players onto the number of teams that will be in that league. Let's use four in this example. Using the evaluation cards to represent players, the top four are selected and placed on the table, one heading up each team. Then, the next best players are added, and so on, until each team has a full complement of players.

The scores of the players on the four teams may look something like this:

12 +	12 +	12	12
10	11	11	11
10	10	10	10
9	9	9	9
7	8	8	8
7	7	7	7
6	6	6	7
4	4	5	5

always before the scheduled time so that when the scheduled evaluation is completed, everyone will have been evaluated and teams can be formed immediately thereafter — while the coaches are present.

During the coaches' training sessions, the coaches become familiar with the evaluation procedure. Each coach is assigned to a "station" to evaluate a particular skill. All the children are permitted to run through the skill several times so that the coach can get an idea of the skill level of the group itself. The coach will then give a score to each child based on how the child compares to the group as a whole, as follows:

Above average	3 points
	2½ points
Average	2 points
	1½ points
Below average	1 point

Any child who is found to be exceptional in a particular skill is given a "3 + ."

BASKETBALL AT PEACHTREE

The basketball program at Peachtree Presbyterian Church
is open to anyone in the community who wants to play.
Our youth leagues stress fundamentals, participation, and
sportsmanship. (The younger children shoot at goals set
at a height appropriate to their size.) Our adult "intramural"
program emphasizes fun, fellowship, and fitness.
Everyone who attends practice will get to play at least half
of every game. All registrants will be evaluated and placed
on teams to ensure equal distribution of ability.
Youth leagues will practice one afternoon each week and play
on Saturdays. Practice will begin the week of November 29.
See the schedule below for specific leagues and details:

League*	Evaluation (Day & Time)	Games played on	Fee**
Boys 7&8	Tues. Nov. 16, 5:00 p.m.	Sat. mornings	$25.00
Boys 9&10	Tues. Nov. 16, 6:30 p.m.	Sat. mornings	$25.00
Boys 11&12	Thur. Nov. 18, 5:00 p.m.	Sat. mornings	$25.00
Boys 13&14	Thur. Nov. 18, 5:00 p.m.	Sat. mornings	$25.00
Boys 15-18	Wed. Nov. 17, 8:30 p.m.	Weeknights	$25.00
Men (18+)	Thur. Nov. 18, 7:00 p.m.	Thurs. nights	$25.00
Girls 8-10	Mon. Nov. 15, 5:00 p.m.	Sat. mornings	$25.00
Girls 11&12	Mon. Nov. 15, 5:00 p.m.	Sat. mornings	$25.00
Girls 13&14	Mon. Nov. 15, 5:00 p.m.	Sat. mornings	$25.00
Women (15+)	Mon. Nov. 15, 7:00 p.m.	Monday nights	$22.00

*Age as of September 1, 1982
** Fee includes jersey, shorts & socks for youth 14 and under; jersey
for 15-18 boys, men and women.

Note: Game schedule listed above is subject to change.
Youth and men's league teams will be limited to 8 players;
women's teams limited to 9 players.
To make sure you get on a team, SIGN UP NOW!
Your fee must accompany your registration. Fees will not be
refunded after Nov. 1st.
Everyone (adults included), except men who played last year,
must be evaluated. If you cannot attend the scheduled
evaluation, call us at least one week in advance for an
alternate time (261 7651).

- -

BASKETBALL AT PEACHTREE
Please use a separate form for each participant.

Name _____ Age _____

Address _____

City _____ Zip _____

Home phone _____ Office phone _____

Please return this form with your check to:
Recreation Peachtree Presbyterian Church, 3434
Roswell Rd, N.W., Atlanta, GA 30363   261 7651

Please check one and
attach fee:

___ 7&8 Boys
___ 9&10 Boys
___ 11&12 Boys
___ 13&14 Boys
___ 15-18 Boys
___ Men (18+)
___ 8-10 Girls
___ 11&12 Girls
___ 13&14 Girls
___ Women
Amt. enclosed $_____

Anything any of the coaches may know about a particular player, such as: "a hustler" or "good ball handler" or "better than we rated him or her on shooting" is mentioned and taken into account in the formation of the teams. During this process, we will also take into account requests by parents for children who are neighbors, schoolmates, or friends to play on the same team if it can be done without putting one team at an advantage or disadvantage. Then, when *all* coaches are convinced that each team is as equal in ability to the others as is possible to make them, the teams are selected by the coaches in a *blind* draw. At this point, if a coach wants to coach his or her own child, and did not happen to draw the team that the child was on, a trade for a comparable player is made.

Each coach is then responsible for calling the players to notify them who their coach is and when the first practice will be held.

I realize that I have taken a lot of space to discuss our evaluation procedure, but I think it is the key to a successful church athletic program. While no evaluation or system for selecting teams is perfect, this one, at least, as far as it is possible for us to determine, gives every team an equal chance to compete from the start.

Rosters

In order to assure that each child will play a minimum of half of every game, we limit the number of players on each team. All youth teams have 8 players. We decide beforehand how many teams we can accommodate in each age group (if two teams, we register only sixteen players; if four teams, thirty-two; if six teams, forty-eight), and we have been fortunate so far in that we have always had sufficient registration to fill each league. In every instance, we have at least two teams in each age group so that they can scrimmage against one another during practice.

In our older age groups which compete against teams from other churches, many of the other teams have more than eight players. In cooperation with one another, we have devised a formula which stipulates the minimum amount of time each player gets to play:

if eight or fewer players, each plays at least half

if nine or ten players, each plays one and one-half quarters

if eleven or more, each plays one full quarter, and enters the game during another quarter

We are convinced, however, that children and parents prefer small rosters so everyone gets more playing and practice time.

Practice and Game Schedules

Our practice and game schedules are also determined before we begin registration. That way, parents will know what days and times their children will be involved in basketball. Unless there are more than four teams in a particular age group, each age group practices at the same time. For instance, all 7 & 8 boys teams practice on Monday afternoons at 4:30 and on Saturday mornings at 9:00. (Once the season begins, games take the place of Saturday practices.) We do this primarily to facilitate carpooling in that our church serves such a large area, and many children travel ten or more miles to participate. In this regard, coaches have no say about the times their players will practice. When they are recruited, they must agree to the already-scheduled times.

Uniforms

We have found that children like to keep their team uniforms, so we include in the registration fee enough to purchase each a basketball jersey (T-shirts for girls), shorts, and sox. When they wear the shirts to school and around the neighborhood, it's good promotion for our program.

Recognition

At the conclusion of each season, we have a youth basketball banquet in which we recognize all of the boys and girls who have participated during the year, and say "thanks" to the coaches. We present no team trophies; in fact, we don't even mention won-lost records. Instead, we present an individual trophy (with team name engraved) to each child.

In addition, during the season, team pictures are taken, which are made available to those who want to purchase them. More importantly, however, we have each team's picture mounted on a plaque, along with the team's and coach's name, and present this to each coach at the banquet. It is the most appreciated memento we have found to recognize the efforts of our coaches.

Recruiting and Training of Coaches

I believe the most important thing that I do in regard to youth sports is in the recruiting and training of coaches. A coach has a great influence on the life of a child, in some instances, even more than a teacher. In our program, a coach not only has the responsibility to help children develop their athletic skills, but also to grow in their relationship with Jesus Christ and with one another. Our coaches are not just interested in developing better athletes, but in developing better people. To see that they do this is my responsibility, and one I take very seriously.

Consequently, I am careful, first of all, in the recruiting of coaches. I sit down and talk with each prospective coach about our sports program and what we want to accomplish through it. Then I extend an invitation to coach to those whom I feel are the most dedicated to the concept of our program. During and after the season I review and evaluate the progress of each coach, not based on his or her won-lost record, but on whether or not the children under his or her care are growing in spirit, mind, and body. Each coach is re-evaluated before being asked to coach again the following year. Sometimes coaches are not invited to coach a second time. I have, even on occasion, replaced a coach during the season when I felt it was in the best interest of the children and the program as a whole.

In regard to training, every coach, even those who have previously coached, are required to attend our training sessions. (Old coaches attend not so much for what they can get, but for what they can *offer* to new coaches.) Over a period of several years, my youth basketball director and I have prepared a "Handbook for Coaches," which outlines those things we think are important in the training of a coach. In it, and in our training sessions, we cover such topics as:

- how a child's attention span varies with age.
- how every child needs to be accepted, regardless of skill level; how "ability" and "worth" are not synonymous.
- how things done well should be applauded, and mistakes made should be the occasion for teaching, not criticizing.
- how children like to be called by their names.
- how children like to be treated as equals; that there should be no "pets."

We encourage each coach to instill in players:

- a sense of responsibility — to attend practice, to be on time, to do their best.
- a positive attitude — toward coaches, teammates, opponents, self.
- unselfishness — be part of a "team."
- patience — with self when he or she fails, and with teammates when they do.

In the handbook and training sessions, we review all of the rules and policies with regard to our program as they affect each age group. There are several modifications, in addition to those mentioned earlier (court dimensions, basket height, free throw line, etc.) which have worked well in our program.

Running Clock: Because there are so many fouls and violations in 7- & 8- and 9- & 10-year-old leagues, we play four ten-minute quarters with a "running" clock. In other words, the clock stops *only* for: time outs, foul shots, any unusual delay. It is not stopped for fouls that are taken out of bounds, jump balls, and violations. During the last two minutes of the second and fourth quarters, however, it is operated as it would normally be, stopping for every referee's whistle. This procedure allows us time to complete a game in about an hour and five minutes, when we allow one minute between quarters and five minutes between halves.

Participation Requirement: To facilitate the requirement that everyone play at least half of every game, we operate as follows:

First Quarter: Any five players may start the quarter and must play the entire quarter unless he or she fouls out or is injured.

Second Quarter: The players who did not play the first quarter must enter the game at the beginning of the second quarter, and play the entire quarter. Players remaining in the game from the first quarter may be substituted for at anytime during the quarter by anyone on the bench.

Third Quarter: Repeat first quarter procedure.

Fourth Quarter: Repeat second quarter procedure.

No Pressing: In our 7-10 and 9-10 age leagues we do not allow a full-court press. As soon as the defensive team secures complete control and possession of the basketball by:

1. a rebound
2. a loose ball
3. after a foul shot attempt is made or missed
4. after a field goal is made
5. after a foul or violation
6. after a time out

the defensive team immediately becomes the offensive team and the offensive team is now on defense. At this time, all players on the defense must clear out of the offensive players backcourt area and retreat to their top of the key to set up their defensive positions.

The offensive team then has ten seconds to cross the half court time line. Once a player with the basketball crosses the line, defensive players may begin their defensive play. On a fast break, a defensive player may pick up the player whenever he or she crosses the time line as long as no pressure is put on the offensive player until he or she crosses the line.

In the handbook and in our training sessions, we discuss how to plan and conduct a practice so that the chil-

DID YOU KNOW...

...that the young people who officiate during your child's games are volunteers? They're part of our Gym Team, a corps of high schoolers who serve their church through volunteering their time and talent in various phases of the recreation ministry.

...that they have undergone training in refereeing, keeping score, and operating the clock? In addition, each has had to pass a written and practical exam in the area in which he or she is working, thereby earning the right to officiate.

...that they will make mistakes? This is a learning experience for them, just like playing basketball is for your child.

...that it is harder to officiate in the younger leagues because when a referee sees a violation such as double-dribble, or traveling, or sees one player foul another, the referee must decide whether it is serious enough to call before blowing the whistle? If every violation and foul were called, there wouldn't be much time left to play.

...that violations and fouls are not called the same on every child? For example, we will call walking on a "good" player more quickly than on one who "shuffles the feet" because he or she is still learning what's allowed and what's not.

...that just like the players, the officials like to be told they performed well? It makes them try even harder next time.

---

dren will get the most from it. We discuss basic ball handling and shooting techniques and how to teach them, review dribbling and passing drills, go over offensive and defensive alignments, talk about strategy. Coaches are encouraged to spend the last part of every practice scrimmaging against another team.

It should be noted that training does not end with these pre-season sessions. Training is continuous throughout the season. Either my youth basketball director or I am always in the gym during practices to assist coaches in whatever way we can.

Training and Certification of Officials

We use volunteer officials in our youth basketball* program. Members of our Gym Team (see chapter 3 on Staff) are trained and certified in how to referee and in how to operate the clock and keep score.

Our training of referees is similar to that of coaches in that we emphasize our philosophy and purpose for youth athletics. As with coaches' training, we have pre-

---

*Volunteers are used up through age 12. We pay referees for Jr. High and High School games.

pared a "Handbook for Officials" which covers aspects of refereeing, keeping score, and operating the clock.

The topics in the handbook and training sessions include:

1. Basic basketball rules
2. Modification of rules for various age groups
3. How to referee
   a. How to put the ball into play
   b. Where to position yourself during the game
   c. What to do when a foul occurs
   d. How to administer free throws
   e. What to do when a violation occurs
   f. Use of whistle and hand signals
4. Duties of scorekeepers and timers
   a. Before the game
   b. During the game
   c. After the game

At the conclusion of the training, which includes extensive on-court officiating in practice game situations, the Gym Team members are required to pass both a written and a practical examination in order to be certified. Scorer/Timers, usually younger Gym Team members, must pass the Scorer/Timer exams. Referees must pass both the Referee exams and the Scorér/Timer exams. Those who are certified receive an attractive official's shirt with either the designation "Referee" or "Scorer/Timer."

We have found that the younger the league, the more difficult the official's job. In older leagues, a violation or foul is clear-cut. You simply blow the whistle and make the call. In younger leagues, it is not that precise. An official has to decide how serious the violation or foul was. Some children, for instance, who are just learning to play may "walk" every time they get the ball. Calling a traveling violation every time they traveled would mean they'd never get to play. Also, some children are more skillful than others. Those who "know better" should be called for traveling when they do, otherwise, they'll develop bad playing habits. That means that a referee in a youth basketball game often has to make a "judgment on a 'judgment.'" Consequently, we try to alert our parents and spectators as to what's going on when they see one call go one way and another one another. The enclosed "Did You Know . . ." sheet is given out at the first pre-season game as a means of educating the fans.

We believe that our Gym Team referees and officials are a great asset to our youth basketball program. This experience not only gives them a splendid opportunity to develop self confidence and poise, it is also a challenging and satisfying way to minister to others through church recreation.

ADULT TEAM SPORTS

Our adult team sports program consists of men's and women's basketball, men's and women's softball, and men's, women's, and co-ed volleyball and they emphasize fun, fellowship, and fitness: fun, in that we take playing more seriously than winning; fellowship, in that we try to provide an opportunity for brothers and sisters in Christ to experience the joy of that kinship through competitive athletics; fitness, in that our program provides an appealing way to exercise on a year-round basis.

As with youth sports, the selection of coaches is critical to the success of an adult athletic program. I invite to coach in our adult leagues those persons who have shown an interest in our recreation ministry as participants, who have demonstrated an appreciation of our philosophy of church athletics, who have exhibited leadership qualities, and who have attained a degree of skill and understanding of the game sufficient to be comfortable "coaching" an adult team.

In the following sections, we'll review our procedure for *evaluating players, drafting teams,* and our *participation policies* for each sport.

MEN'S AND WOMEN'S BASKETBALL

Evaluation: Our evaluation of adults is not as formal as with youth. Those who played the previous year are not required to be re-evaluated as their coaches will have evaluated each at the end of the previous season.

At the time of the evaluation, we introduce the coaches, give an overview of our program and explain the purpose of the evaluation. We then ask four players at a time to come down to the other end of the gym and let the coaches watch them shoot some jump shots and layups. From this, we can see their jumping ability, shooting techniques and accuracy, ball handling skill and height.

The coaches sit together and come up with a consensus score on each as follows:

5 + = Outstanding player, one of the best
5   = Excellent player
4   = Good player
3   = Average player
2   = Below average player
1   = Poor player

Drafting: When all players have been evaluated their names are written on a blackboard in order of their scores. The decision as to who will draft first, and who second, and so on, is made by a draw.

If there were six teams being formed, the drafting would follow this order:

MEMO

TO: COACHES IN MEN'S AND WOMEN'S BASKETBALL LEAGUES

FROM: BILL MANESS   261-7651

SUBJECT: YOUR RESPONSIBILITIES

1. Call your players to let them know:

    a. You are their coach
    b. Their team "number" or "letter" (see below)
    c. When they will practice

2. With your team, decide on a name for it and report it
    to me no later than December 3.

TEAM NAMES AND LETTERS

Team Number	Men	Team Letter	Women
1	Bunte	A	Maness
2	Kayes	B	Bourne
3	C. Cavanagh	C	Newton
4	Riggs	D	Staples
5	M. Cavanagh		
6	Hamner		

PRACTICE SCHEDULE

MEN				WOMEN			
Thurs. Nov. 29	6:30	1 & 2		Mon. Nov. 26	7:00	A & B	
	7:45	3 & 4			8:15	C & D	
	9:00	5 & 6					
				Mon. Dec. 3	7:00	C & A	
Thurs. Dec. 6	6:30	3 & 5			8:15	D & B	
	7:45	6 & 2					
	9:00	1 & 4		Mon. Dec. 10	7:00	D & B	
					8:15	A & C	
Thurs. Dec. 13	6:30	6 & 4					
	7:45	5 & 1					
	9:00	2 & 3					

Note: During each practice, another team will also be on the
court. You may want to spend the first part of the time on
fundamentals and the last part with a scrimmage. Your use of
the time is up to you.

1st round	2nd round	3rd round	4th round
Coach #1	Coach #6	Coach #1	Coach #6
Coach #2	Coach #5	Coach #2	Coach #5
Coach #3	Coach #4	Coach #3	Coach #4
Coach #4	Coach #3	Coach #4	Coach #3
Coach #5	Coach #2	Coach #5	Coach #2
Coach #6	Coach #1	Coach #6	Coach #1

and so one, until all players are drafted.

Participation: In our adult basketball program we limit the team rosters to eight players in the men's league and nine players in the women's.

We employ the following policy to assure that everyone gets to play a minimum of half of each game: Half way through each quarter, the game is stopped and those who did not play in the first half of the quarter play the remainder of that quarter. Note, a coach may begin any quarter with any five players.

Organization: At the time of the draft, I give to each coach a memo stating responsibilities and indicating the practice times that have been scheduled for his or her team. I also hand out a copy of our rules and regulations as listed below:

1. *High School Rules*
   Current Georgia State High School Rules will govern play except as modified herein.

2. *Participation Requirement*
   All players present are required to play a minimum of half of the game. In order to facilitate this requirement, the following policy has been established: Half way through each quarter the game will be stopped, and anyone who did not play in the first half of the quarter will play the remainder of that quarter.

3. *Forfeit*
   A team must have at least four players dressed and ready to play no later than ten minutes after the scheduled time for the first game and no later than five minutes after the scheduled time for the second and third game.

4. *Technical Fouls*
   Use of profanity will result in a technical foul. Two technical fouls will automatically eject a player from the game.

5. *Protests*
   Decision of the officials will be final.

6. *Enforcement of Rules*
   The Sports Sub-Committee of the Recreation Committee has the authority to interpret, further modify, enforce the rules of this league, and rule on matters not specifically covered herein.

Clinic for Women: Prior to the evaluation, we run a basketball clinic for two nights for those women who have registered who want to brush up on their shooting and ball handling skills.

Men's and Women's Softball

Our "Softball at Peachtree" information sheet (on page 37) describes in detail our softball program.

Evaluation: Our evaluation system is similar to the one we use for basketball. At the time of evaluation we introduce the coaches, thank the participants for registering, and explain that we want to watch them hit and field so that we may distribute their ability evenly on the teams. We use the same scoring system — 1, 2, 3, 4, 5, 5+ — as in basketball, to evaluate "hitting" and "fielding." Hitting consists of taking cuts at about ten pitches; fielding consists of taking ground balls at short and throwing to first or receiving fly balls in center and throwing to second and home, depending on their preference of infield or outfield. We also ask each player the position they prefer to play, and those who want to pitch are allowed to toss some to the hitters so that we can observe their technique and control.

Drafting: When all players have been evaluated, their names, along with those who played the previous year, are arranged on a master list according to their composite score (average of hitting and fielding). Position preference is also noted. A copy of this list is given to each coach, and the drafting begins and proceeds as in basketball.

Participation: The number of players on both our men's and women's softball teams is limited to fifteen. Our participation policy provides that at the top of the fourth inning, those players who did not start will enter the game and play through the sixth inning. A coach then has the prerogative of leaving those players in the game or reinserting the original players at the top of the seventh inning.

Organization: At the time of the draft a booklet containing a roster of coaches with phone numbers, the "Rules, Regulations & Policies" of the league, a memo to the coaches with instructions, and a practice schedule, is given to each coach. A copy of the memo is included herein to give you an idea of the organizational aspects of running a softball league. The rules are listed below.

Rules: National Federation Softball Rules govern play except as provided below:

MEMO

TO: SOFTBALL COACHES

FROM: BILL MANESS

We appreciate your willingness to coach one of our softball teams. Be assured that I am ready at all times to assist you in any way that I can. The following information should be helpful:

1. EQUIPMENT A bag containing bats and balls has been provided for you. Men's coaches have: 4 aluminum bats (32, 33, 34, 34), 1 wooden bat and 8 balls. Women's coaches have: 4 aluminum bats (30, 31, 32, 33) and 6 balls.

A number (1-8) or a letter (A-D) on the bag corresponds to the number or letter of your team.

Please take care of the equipment and return it to me promptly after the season is over.

2. PRACTICE TIMES See attached schedule. Practice times have been made available at Garden Hills school field. To reserve times call the Recreation office (261-7651) any weekday between 9:00-2:00.

3. PERMISSION TO USE FIELD We have permission from the Board of Education at Garden Hills school to use the field at the times designated on the attached schedule. When you arrive at the field for practice, you may find the field is in use. You should inform the person in charge that the field has been scheduled for our use at that time. I have enclosed a copy of the permit to use the field which you can present if necessary.

Remember we are using the field at the pleasure of the school and/or Board of Education. Please encourage your players and spectators to keep the grounds clean and respect the property in every way.

4. LIGHTS AT GARDEN HILLS If you plan to practice after dark at Garden Hills, come by the Recreation office on that day to pick up a key to the switchbox. The key must be returned to the Recreation office the following day.

5. ASSISTANT COACHES You may select whomever you wish to be your assistant coach. Please call us and let us know whom you select.

6. GAME SCHEDULE If for any reason you cannot play on a particular night (this applies to men's teams only), or if you prefer a particular time on a given night (6:30 or 8:00 p.m.), please notify the Recreation office by noon on April 30th.

7. RULES A copy of league rules and ground rules for the field is enclosed. You are expected to know them and instruct your players accordingly.

1. The home team will be determined by a flip of the coin at the time the coaches meet with the umpires prior to the start of the game. At that time the umpires will go over ground rules with the coaches.

2. Each player must play three consecutive innings. At the beginning of the fourth inning, players who did not start the game must enter and play through the sixth inning. At the beginning of the seventh inning, the original players may re-enter the game provided that each bats in the position of the player for whom he or she is substituted.

3. Each coach is responsible for giving the lineup to the scorekeeper (or umpire) prior to the game. All players (including subsitutes) must be listed on the lineup card.

4. A team must have at least eight eligible players ready to play no later than ten minutes after the stated starting time or the game will be forfeited. Players arriving after the start of the game must wait until the end of a half inning before entering the game and must be placed at the end of the batting order.

5. Safety Rules: A runner who deliberately runs into a fielder who is holding the ball waiting to make tag will be automatically out and will be removed from the game.

A player faking a tag without the ball shall be removed from the game.

Any attempt to break up a double play by interfering with the fielder will result in the baserunner being called out and the next runner who has advanced nearest to home being called out.

6. No inning will begin more than an hour and thirty minutes after the start of the game unless the game is tied.

7. Warmup area for players playing in the second game will be to the right of the poles down the rightfield line.

8. We are allowing a full 1½ hours for each game. It is necessary therefore, that we begin on time. Infield practice will not be permitted after the scheduled starting time of a game.

9. No smoking or drinking will be permitted on the field, in the coaches' box, or on the team bench.

10. Neither Peachtree Presbyterian Church nor Garden Hills School assumes any responsibility for injuries to players or spectators.

11. In case of rain, the coaches (not the players) should call the church (261-7651) between 4:00 and 5:00 P.M. to determine if the game for that day has been called. If it has not been called by 4:00 P.M., the decision to play or postpone will be made at the field at game time. The players should, therefore, show up at the field ready to play; otherwise the game will be forfeited. Rained out games will be rescheduled on Wednesday nights.

12. The Recreation Committee has the authority to interpret, further modify, and enforce the rules of this league, including authority on matters not specifically covered herein.

MEN'S, WOMEN'S, AND CO-ED VOLLEYBALL

Our volleyball program is run similarly to our other adult sports programs. We have men's and women's volleyball running concurrently during the fall, prior to basketball season; co-ed volleyball is played in the late winter and early spring, between the basketball and softball seasons.

Evaluation and drafting procedures follow the pattern for adult sports. Teams are limited to nine players. Six at a time; those not in the game rotate in at the change of service.

Sunday School Volleyball

I want to share with you the most exciting adult athletic program — from the standpoint of enthusiasm, participation, and fun — that we've ever done at Peachtree. It's called Sunday School Volleyball. It took a lot of promotion the first time around. Now people are always asking, "When are we going to play Sunday School Volleyball again?"

We call it Sunday School Volleyball because the adult Sunday school classes compete against one another. Each class fields a team; larger classes may have two or more.

The secret of its success is in the "modification" of the rules of the game that permits *everyone* to really get involved and become an integral part of the team. Read the information sheet carefully. It's a "super" way to play co-ed volleyball that minimizes age and ability and makes teamwork paramount.

GOLF

We have found that golf appeals to many who do not care for team sports. I've included the information sheet on our annual golf tournament. As you can see, we are not trying to establish who is the church champion, but rather to enjoy Christian fellowship, make new friends, and have a good time.

SUNDAY SCHOOL VOLLEYBALL

Sunday School volleyball is a program of "modified" co-ed volleyball in which Sunday school classes compete against one another.

The "modification" makes it possible for everyone to be involved in the game.

1. You may have as many players as you wish, but only 6, 7, 8, or 9 may be in the game at any one time. Others may rotate in at each service break.

If more than 12 people want to play from a class, that class should form more than one team: Seekers I, Seekers II, etc.

2. If there are 6 players on the court, at least 2 must be women; if there are 7 or 8, at least 3 must be women; if there are 9, at least 4 must be women.

3. Each time the ball comes into your court, it must be volleyed by a woman before it goes back over the net.

4. Spiking is not permitted; the ball must be hit UP every time.

5. Serves are to be underhand only.

6. After 5 points are scored, the serve goes to the other team.

7. Games last for a specified period of time (10 minutes, for example). Play begins with the sound of a horn and continues until the horn sounds again. The team records the total number of points it scored during the playing period. After a brief rest period, teams change opponents and play begins again.

8. Games will be played on Monday nights and Thursday nights, if needed. Teams play only one night per week from 8:00 until 9:30.

9. The season will last for four weeks, beginning the week of March 17th.

_ _
Please return this form to Bill Maness

_____class will have _____ team(s).

The person in charge is _____

Home phone _____   Office phone _____

<u>GOLF TOURNAMENT INFORMATION</u>

I'm delighted that you're going to play in our first Peachtree Golf Tournament. The following information should tell you what you need to know, but if you have any questions, don't hesitate to call me at 261-7651.

<u>PLACE:</u> The tournament will be played at Rivermont Golf & Country Club. Rivermont may be reached by taking Ga. 400 north to Holcomb Bridge Road, east on Holcomb Bridge approximately 3½ miles to Nesbitt Ferry, north on Nesbitt Ferry for ½ mile to Rivermont Parkway which you will follow to the clubhouse.

<u>START:</u> We will be using a "shotgun" start, which means everyone will tee-off <u>exactly</u> at 12:30. It is imperative, therefore, that you arrive at the clubhouse no later than <u>11:50</u> so that you can pay the $10.00 balance due, get your cart assignment, meet your foursome, and position yourself at the proper tee so that you can begin at the sound of the gun.

Sandwiches will be available at 11:30; however, if you want to eat at the clubhouse, please call the church and let us know.

<u>PLAY:</u> We will be using the Lauderdale or "scramble" method of play. Each foursome, which should contain an "A," "B," "C," and "D" player (based on the estimated score you recorded on the application form), will play as a team.

After you tee-off, each player will move his or her ball to the point where the best drive ended up. All players will then shoot a second shot from that spot. This process will be repeated for <u>every</u> shot, including the putts. All lies may be improved except in a trap, in which case other players will drop a ball. Once a player has holed-out, other putts need not be shot. Keep your team's score and turn it in at the conclusion of play.

<u>CLOSEST TO THE PIN AND LONGEST DRIVE:</u> Men's and women's markers will be provided to record the longest drives and closest to the pin. If your ball lands farther from the tee (in the fairway) on hole #2 or closer to the pin on hole #6, place your name at the bottom of the card attached to the marker and move it to the point where your ball landed.

<u>PURPOSE:</u> We are not trying to establish a church champion but rather to enjoy Christian fellowship, make new friends, and have a good time. Let us know what you think about what we've done. Perhaps we will want to do this more often than once a year.

<u>AWARDS:</u> Awards for various categories will be presented on the clubhouse balcony immediately after the completion of the tournament. Yes, snacks will be available on a cash basis.

SEE YOU ON TUESDAY, MAY 30th, BY 11:50 <u>AT THE LATEST</u>.

                                                    BILL

Sports at Peachtree

The following statement, summary, and calendar of the athletic activities offered at Peachtree is presented as an overview of our program to be used as a guide in the development of your sports ministry.

We believe that you don't have to be young and athletic to enjoy participating in sports. Consequently, our sports program at Peachtree is open to both members and non-members who want to participate, regardless of age or ability. We do ask, however, that each person who has not participated in a particular sport at Peachtree be evaluated in that sport so that we can determine his or her ability. In that way, we can equally distribute ability to each team.

Our youth leagues emphasize fundamentals, participation, and sportsmanship. In our adult leagues, the emphasis is on fun, fellowship, and fitness. All of our adult leagues and many of our youth teams play on an intramural basis; that is, all of the teams in the league are from our own church. Fees are charged to cover direct costs, such as: uniforms, officials, equipment, and field maintenance.

So that you can make youir plans to participate, the following *calendar* and *summary* of our athletic activities is offered. Detailed information on each activity will appear in the weekly bulletin allowing ample time for you to register. Although members are given priority in registering, it is wise to register early as most leagues fill up completely.

SPORTS SUMMARY

Co-ed Pickup Volleyball	Open to anyone who drops in. Every Tuesday night throughout the year, 8:00-10:00 P.M. No fee.
Men's Volleyball	A competitive league open to men 16 years and older. Thursday nights. Mid-September through October. Registration required.
Women's Volleyball	A competitive league open to women 15 years and older. Monday nights. Mid-September through October. Registration required.
Co-ed Volleyball	A modified game in which women are required to volley the ball before it is returned over the net. Spiking and overhand serving are not permitted. Sixteen years and older. Monday nights. Early March through mid-April. Registration required.
Youth Basketball	Open to boys 7-18 and girls 8-14 years of age. Practice on weekday afternoons and games on Saturdays. Older boys play on weeknights. Mid-November through February. Registration required.
Men's Basketball	A competitive league for men 18 years and older. Practice and games on Thursday nights. Late November through February. Registration required.
Women's Basketball	A competitive league for women 15 years of age and older. Practice and games on Monday nights. Late November through February. Registration required.
Golf Tournaments	Two tournaments are held during the year — one in the fall and one in the spring. Varying handicapping systems are used. Open to all Peachtree members and their friends. Registration required.
Men's Softball	A competitive league open to men 15 years and older. Practice and games on Monday and Thursday nights. Mid-April through mid-July. Registration required.
Women's Softball	A competitive league open to women 15 years and older. Practice and games on Tuesday nights. Mid-April through mid-July. Registration required.
Youth Basketball Camp	A camp for boys and girls covering basic basketball skills. Late summer. Registration required.

SPORTS CALENDAR

	Sep	Oct	Nov	Dec	Jan	Feb	Mar	Apr	May	Jun	Jul	Aug
Co-ed Pickup Volleyball	V V V	V V V	V V V	V V V	V V V	V V V	V V V	V V V	V V V	V V V	V V V	V V V
Men's Volleyball		MV	MV MV									
Women's Volleyball		WV	WV WV									
Co-ed Volleyball							CV CV	CV CV CV				
Youth Basketball			YB YB	YB YB	YB YB	YB						
Men's Basketball			MB	MB MB	MB MB	MB						
Women's Basketball				WB WB	WB WB	WB						
Golf Tournaments		G							G			
Men's Softball								MS MS	MS MS	MS MS		
Women's Softball								WS WS	WS WS	WS WS		
Youth Basketball Camp												YBC

7

FACILITIES:
Building for Programming

So, you're at the point in the development of your church's recreation ministry when it is time to start thinking about building a facility. Hopefully, you already have an established recreation program, limited though it may be, for a facility should be the natural extension of an already existing ministry. Without such a program in operation to serve as a base, it would be difficult to make intelligent decisions about the needs for a facility. Having an on-going program is a prerequisiste for assessing building needs and for determining what you want in the way of a facility.

In this chapter, we'll give you some guidelines for assessing your needs as we examine the various "space" requirements for a variety of recreation activities. In addition, we will make some specific recommendations about the design of such "spaces," which are the result of personal experience and conversations with others who have had the opportunity to conduct programs in all kinds of "spaces." In other words, we want to help you decide what you want (need) in your facility, and then suggest some things which will enhance the utilization of each "space." We will do this on a space-by-space basis, looking at such spaces as: a gym, all-purpose room, game room, craft room, control counter, etc.

To begin with, however, I want to mention two things which will be an integral part of our look at individual spaces: the *type of facility* you want to build and *control.* Then at the conclusion of this chapter, we'll discuss some general concerns with regard to building operation from a planning and design standpoint.

Type of Facility

Just what kind of facility do you have in mind? In this regard, you may want to consider your overall church program needs, for a recreation facility need not be limited to recreation. In fact, a multi-use facility, in light of the cost of construction, may be something your church would want to think about.

When funds are limited, multi-use design may enable you to have education and fellowship as well as recreation possibilities in the same facility. Classrooms which can be used for recreation classes on weekdays can serve as church school rooms on Sunday. A gymnasium can double as a dining/fellowship hall. The multiple use of space will add new dimensions to maintenance and operation, and that should be considered in your decision on whether or not to build for multi-use. In our space-by-space discussion, we'll bring these to light to help you weigh the pros and cons of multi-use areas.

Control

In my opinion, and that of most of the recreation directors with whom I've talked, the primary consideration in the design of any recreation facility is *control.* Control, in this case, means the capacity to monitor and influence what goes on in your building.

If you have any doubts about the need for control, just put a handful of kids in a gym full of balls or in a game room with bumperpool equipment, and turn your back for fifteen minutes. If you haven't had the experience, you'd be amazed at what can happen during innocent play. It would seem that balls were made for kicking into lights and pool cues designed for poking out ceiling panels.

To a greater or lesser degree, adult "play," too, needs some control. Play is an activity in which it's appropriate to exercise less restraint than usual, but someone needs to be able to see that play doesn't get out of hand. Control is needed anytime a recreation facility is in use, but particularly during "open" periods when persons are encouraged to "do their own thing."

How do you achieve control? There are two ways: The first is through *sight* and *sound*. Therefore, a recreation facility must be designed so that the person on duty can monitor what is going on with both eyes and ears. Plans should be drawn in such a way as to insure that a supervising attendant can see and hear virtually everything that is happening in a building, especially in those areas which will be "open" at certain times.

The second way to achieve control is through traffic flow. A recreation facility should be designed so that there is only one entrance, and everyone entering the building can be seen and greeted by the attendant on duty. In addition, it should be possible to close off certain areas of the building when they are not in use.

The importance of control cannot be overemphasized. It is the key to the safe and efficient operation of a recreation building. During our discussion of various spaces, I will reiterate the importance of control and provide guidelines for achieving it. Suffice it to say at this point that control must be an integral part of the planning and ultimate design of a building. The building design must lend itself to control; it cannot be added on after the building is finished.

Spaces

In this section, we'll look at the various programming and adjunct areas that may be incorporated into a recreation facility. You will want to study each to determine whether it is a requisite to the implementation of your church's recreation ministry.

GYMNASIUM

A gymnasium is the "space" that most churches consider essential in planning a recreation facility. It is certainly indispensable if your ministry will include the two most popular indoor participation sports: basketball and volleyball. This "room for sports" as it has been called, will also provide for other sports: badminton, rollerskating, paddle tennis, one-wall raquetball, gymnastics, tumbling, etc. In addition, it will be used for a myriad of activities for both children and adults: games, exercise classes, square dancing, jogging, just to mention a few. Because your gymnasium will easily be the most used space in your recreation facility — both from the standpoint of scheduled activities and "open" periods — more thought and planning should go into its design than that of any other area in your building.

Size: The most important consideration is size. It's easy to say that a gym should be 80' by 100', as is sometimes done, and let it go at that. Such a cursory approach fails to take into consideration what *use* will be made of the gym and the fact that a gym must be designed to *accommodate standard playing court dimensions*. Let's look at various gym sizes based on these two criteria: use and court dimensions.

A standard senior high school basketball court is 50' in width by 84' in length. Thus the absolute *minimum size* for a gym, allowing 6 feet around the periphery of the court for safety purposes and for team benches and spectators' chairs would be 62' by 96'. (See diagram #1.) Note that the court is shifted toward one side of the gym to allow more room on the side where players and spectators sit.

Youth basketball games could also be played on this court, although it would be a bit large, by installing height-adjustable backboards. (Height adjustable backboards are a must for youth basketball.) There would also be adequate room for one volleyball court (30' × 60') inside the basketball court. A gym of this size would accommodate all of the activities mentioned above.

By adding 10' to the width of the gym (72' × 96'), you can practically double its usefulness. You would then have room for two youth-size basketball courts (38' × 66') and two volleyball courts. (See diagram #2.)

Having two youth basketball courts is imperative if you plan to have a significant youth basketball program. With two courts you can practice four teams at one time, and you can have two games going at one time. (Two games can easily be played simultaneously on adjacent courts without interfering with one another. You will find that the referees whistles and the operation of two clocks will not be confusing to the players or spectators.)

Two volleyball courts are also highly desirable, in that you can accommodate twice as many players, and you can run tournaments that would otherwise not be possible.

There are two problems with a court this size, however. There is minimum spectator space for youth games, and you will have more spectators for youth basketball games than for any other activity. Also, it will be necessary to install on the main court swing-up type backboards which will have to be moved out of the way anytime youth basketball games are being played, as they will project into the playing courts.

Both of these problems can be solved by adding an additional 18' to the length of the gym (making it 72' ×

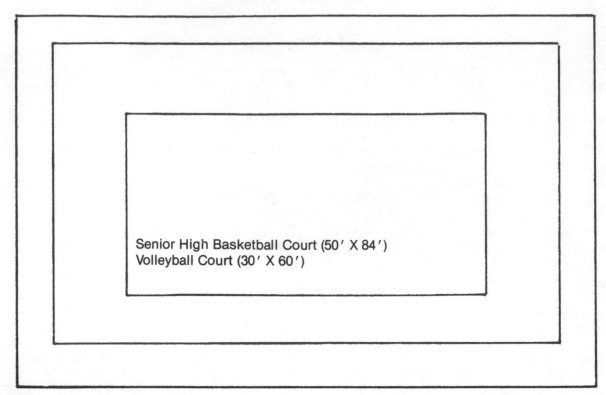

Senior High Basketball Court (50′ X 84′)
Volleyball Court (30′ X 60′)

Diagram #1
GYM (62′ X 96′)

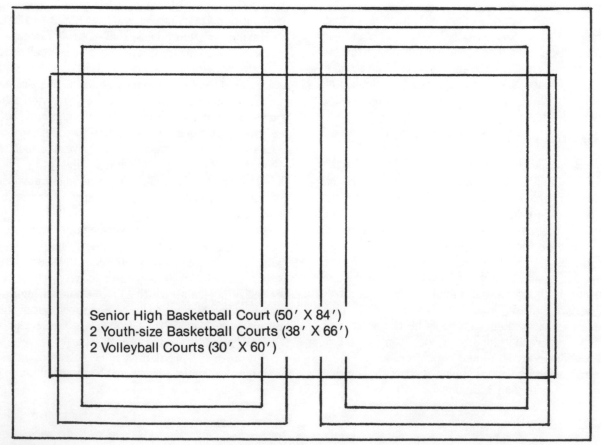

Senior High Basketball Court (50′ X 84′)
2 Youth-size Basketball Courts (38′ X 66′)
2 Volleyball Courts (30′ X 60′)

Diagram #2
GYM (72′ X 96′)

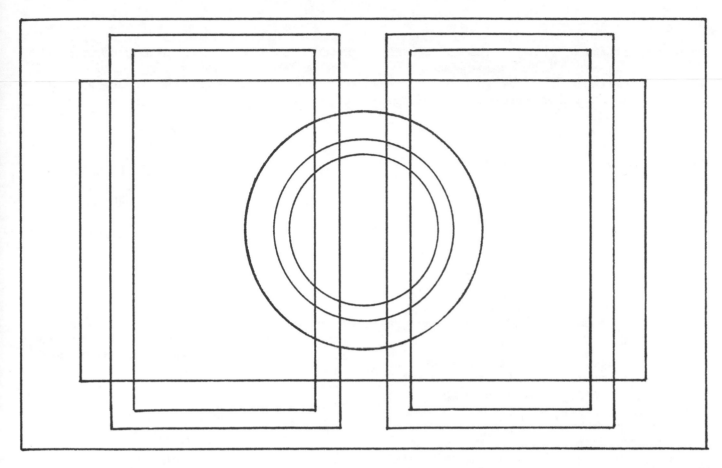

Diagram #3
GYM (72′ X 114′)

NCAA Basketball Court (50′ X 94′)
2 Youth-size Basketball Courts (38′ X 66′)
2 Volleyball Courts (30′ X 60′)

114′). This size gym would then accommodate the more desirable NCAA basketball court (50′ × *94′*), but more importantly, give you the space to have two adjacent youth-sized courts which could be used without interference from the goals on the main court. (See diagram #3.)

Two volleyball courts will fit into the youth-sized basketball courts. In this case, in order to play volleyball without hinderance from the side baskets, it will be necessary to install swing-away backboards on the sides.

A gym of this size (72′ × *114′*) is the most functional size possible for the cost of construction. Every square foot is usable. Standard playing courts can be laid-out without crowding, and there will still be adequate space for spectators.

Ceiling Height: Ceiling height should be a minimum of 24′. Anything less will hinder the playing of volleyball, and it will have an adverse visual effect, as well.

Floor: It is highly recommended that a gymnasium have a "floating" floor, one in which the sub-flooring rests on rubber pads. This allows the floor to "give" when it is played on, cushioning the impact on an athlete's legs and feet when running and jumping. The floor surface should be hard maple, preferably installed in a parquet fashion. Such a floor will prove to be highly durable, easy to maintain, and it will provide a surface compatible with virtually any activity, including roller-skating.

Basketball Goals: The main basketball goals should

be the ceiling-mounted, backward swing-up type with rectangular, tempered glass backboards. Manual operation is sufficient in a $72' \times 114'$ gym, as they will seldom have to be moved. In a smaller gym, where they may have to be raised often, a power winch is recommended. The secondary (side) goals should be the wall-mounted, swing-away type with height adjustment and steel, fan-shaped backboards. If your gym will not have youth-sized courts, the height-adjustment feature should be included on the main goals.

Wall Pads: Protective wall pads should be installed on the walls under each goal. Tumbling mats that can be attached to the wall with a Velcro strip can double as wall padding.

Doors: All gym doors should open *away* from the gym. Entrance doors should have a vertical safety glass panel so that persons, including children, entering the gym can see through them.

Court Markings: The various playing areas (main basketball court, secondary basketball courts, volleyball courts) should be lined in bold colors. It is recommended that complete lanes, not just foul lines, be marked on secondary basketball courts.

In addition, I have a personal recommendation for marking. I would suggest that three concentric circles, whose centers are the center of the main basketball court, be drawn at 12', 15', and 20' radiuses. (See diagram #3.) This will greatly facilitate getting children and even high school youth in a circle for games and activities requiring such a formation. Each should be a different color. They will not interfere with other activities in the gym.

Floor Plates: Purchase your volleyball standards before your gym floor is completed so that installation of floor plates can be coordinated with installation of the floor. Depending on the type you get, they may need to be mounted in the concrete slab before it is poured.

Storage: Adequate storage adjacent to the gym is a must. It should have *extra large doors* which provide an entrance near the middle of the room so that equipment can be easily rolled in and out. You will need room for volleyball standards, chairs and/or portable bleachers, tumbling mats, gymnastic equipment, etc. The storage room should be large enough for you to get any item of equipment in or out without having to disturb anything else.

Air Circulation: Air conditioning a gym is virtually prohibitive from the standpoint of cost and energy consumption. Well designed air-handling equipment, on the other hand, will suffice even on hot days and nights *if* it will circulate the air at the floor level. Most air distribution systems merely circulate the air near the ceiling. Be sure to stress to your architect the importance of ventilation at floor level.

Lights: High intensity discharge (HID) lights are recommended as they give more light per watt, and they generally have a longer life than incandescent lights. The fixtures should be highly durable, as they will inevitably get hit by balls. Gym lights should be wired so that they are controlled from a panel box that can be locked. Also, it should be possible to turn on the lights over one-half of the gym when the other half is not in use.

Scoreboards: Scoreboards should be installed high enough that they are not likely to be hit by errant balls and that they can readily be seen by players and spectators. The control cable should be installed to permit operation near mid-court.

If you have two youth basketball courts, a scoreboard should be provided for each. One of the two should be operable from the mid courts of both the main and secondary courts.

Visibility: For control purposes, a gym should be highly visible from other areas of the building. Large windows should be included in the design of a gym. They should be located in lobby areas and also upstairs (if your facility has a second floor) so that the attendant on duty can maintain visual contact from various parts of the building.

Structural Steel: Structural steel supports that protrude into the gym area pose a safety hazard. They should be recessed into the gym walls.

Clock: A clock in the gym will greatly facilitate the operation of classes and other activities on schedule.

Electrical Outlets: At least two electrical outlets should be placed on each wall of the gym. There'll be more occasions than you can imagine in which they'll be needed.

Dining/Fellowship: If your gymnasium must double as a dining/fellowship hall, your architect should pay particular attention to acoustics, which are usually not good in gymnasiums. Also give careful consideration to selecting a floor which can be easily cleaned and is impervious to water, and one that will be resistant to scratches from tables and chairs.

In addition, extra storage space adjacent to the area should be provided as it will be necessary to completely remove tables and chairs for athletic activities. Note, too, that alternating setups for dining and recreation will take time and necessitate careful scheduling to avoid conflicts.

LOCKER ROOMS

Shower, locker, and dressing facilities for men and women are indispensable if you have a gymnasium. Two individual shower stalls for women and a shower area with four showers for men will likely be adequate. The number of lockers you will need will depend on whether most of those using your facility come dressed to play or whether they come in their business clothes. In a suburban church, four to six lockers for women and sixteen to twenty for men should be sufficient. In a downtown facility, with heavy noontime drop-in participation, more may be needed. Dressing areas are not usually air conditioned because of the high humidity in them. It is important, therefore, that adequate air circulation equipment be installed. Very few architects recommend an air exchange system that is sufficient. Be sure that yours does.

An epoxy floor finish in the wet areas may be more economical than ceramic tile. It should be properly installed, however, to assure that there is adequate texture to provide a non-slippery surface.

ALL-PURPOSE ROOM

Probably the second most used space in your facility will be an all-purpose room. This room will often serve as an auxiliary gymnasium, as it will frequently be used for those classes where movement is involved, such as exercise and dance, as well as children's games and activities. In addition, it will give you needed space for quiet activities involving a large number of people.

Such a room should be a minimum of 1400 square feet, preferably 2000 square feet or more. It takes about 50-60 square feet per person for exercise and dance classes. A 1400 square foot room will comfortably accommodate about twenty-five persons for dance or exercise. This room should have a tile (not carpeted) floor. One or more large storage closets should be adjacent. Such a room would logically be located on the second floor of a two-story facility.

GAME ROOM

The next largest room in your building should be a game room. Such a name is a misnomer, however, since it's a waste of valuable space not to plan for this room to double as a classroom.

It should be 800-1000 square feet in size, and should be located on the main floor, across from the control counter so that activities during "open" periods can be monitored by the attendant on duty. Control will be greatly enhanced if the wall facing the control counter is made of glass. Draw drapes should be installed across the glass to provide privacy when the room is being used as a classroom. Again, adjacent storage is important. This room should be carpeted, primarily to make it quieter.

YOUTH LOUNGE

You may want to provide a "youth" lounge in your facility. This room which will also be used as a medium-size classroom, would be designed as a "meeting" room for high school young people. Approximately 600 square feet in size, this room could be carpeted and furnished with sofas, comfortable chairs, and, perhaps, a piano.

CRAFT ROOM

A rugged room will be needed in your facility if you plan to have crafts which involve paint or ceramics. This room should be equipped with sturdy, old tables, which will provide a surface for working on craft projects. An adjacent, but separate, workroom — with a sink, cabinets, space for a kiln, and storage for unfinished craft projects — which can be locked will enable the craft room to double as a classroom. The craft room and work room combined should be around 600 square feet in size and have a rubber or vinyl tile floor. Be sure to provide adequate wiring for a kiln.

CLASSROOMS

Additional classrooms are an asset to any recreation facility. They will provide you with the opportunity to offer a varied and extensive potpourri of classes and activities. Each room should be approximately 350 to 400 square feet in size, have tiled floors, and contain wall-mounted blackboards. If possible, two adjacent rooms should be equipped with a movable divider so that they can be made into one.

CONTROL COUNTER

An enclosed counter that is strategically placed is essential for maintaining control in your facility. The counter should be located so that the attendant on duty can see into the gymnasium and game room, and also have a view of the entrance. Ideally, the control counter will be an integral part of the main lobby, situated in such a manner that persons entering the building will naturally be inclined to move to it. A telephone for incoming calls should be located at the control counter.

EQUIPMENT ROOM

An equipment room should be located directly behind the control counter. This room will be used for storing small athletic equipment, such as basketballs, volleyballs, and rollerskates. It should have ample shelving, and if rollerskates are to be stored, the shelves should be sloped toward the front so that the skates line up evenly when placed on the shelves. In our equipment room, we maintain an old school desk with a vise attached and an assortment of tools and spare parts in the drawers so that the attendant can repair skates and other equipment during slack times.

SECRETARY'S OFFICE

The secretary's office should, like the control counter, be located so that she or he can see the gym, game room, lobby, and entrance to the facility. The walls of the office adjacent to the lobby should be made of glass. To facilitate communication, I would recommend that a set of pigeonhole mail boxes (one for each instructor) be located in the secretary's office so that messages between instructors and the secretary can be readily exchanged.

DIRECTOR'S OFFICE

The director's office, should, if possible, be located off the "beaten path." Otherwise, everyone dropping in to use the facility will be inclined to stop in for a chat. While the director's office should *always* be open to everyone, he or she will never get anything accomplished if the office is immediately visible. A closet should be included in the director's office.

In our facility, the director's office is on the second floor, overlooking the entrance to the building. There is also a view of the gymnasium through the office door. Such a location provides a degree of control when others are not on duty.

KITCHEN

A small kitchen will enhance the use of your facility. It should be located next to the all-purpose room. Be sure to include a pantry adjacent to the kitchen.

LOBBIES

A lobby on each level of your facility is desirable both from the standpoint of practicality and aesthetics. A lobby lends a pleasant degree of "openness" to the facility and provides a place for people to congregate before, during, and after participating in classes and activities. As many rooms as possible should open into the lobby(ies).

CONCESSION AREA

An area on the main floor, in view of the control counter, should be designated for vending machines.

JANITOR'S CLOSETS

A janitor's closet with a large wash basin should be located on each floor of your facility.

GENERAL ITEMS

Attention to the following items will improve upon the operation of your facility:

Light Switches: Lights should be controlled through conveniently placed wall switches (except for the gymnasium) — instead of a panel box — so they can be turned on and off as needed.

Electrical Outlets: A sufficient number of electrical outlets should be provided in all rooms to accommodate movie projectors, phonographs, etc.

Water Fountains: Water fountains should be located close to the gym and in each locker room. If your facility has a second story, one should be provided there, too.

Air Conditioning: A separate system for the director's and secretary's offices will enable you to cool only those areas when other parts of the building are not in use. In addition, multiple systems throughout the building will permit selected cooling of areas in use.

Sound System: A sound system is expensive and of little value in an ordinary recreation facility. A good portable sound system will more than do the job in any foreseeable circumstance.

Access for the Handicapped: Your building should be designed to provide for the handicapped.

Thermostat Covers: All thermostat controls should have sturdy, metal, lockable covers to prevent tampering.

Signs: Signs designating room names and/or numbers should be included in the design of the building.

Bulletin Board: A bulletin board should be located in the main lobby so that persons entering the building will see it.

Telephones: Some church recreation facilities have a separate phone line. We have found it quite satisfactory to have existing lines from the church run to the recreation building. That way, all calls for recreation go through the church receptionist. Thus, if no one happens to be in the recreation facility, the calls will still be answered. When the receptionist leaves in the afternoon, a switch near the control counter can be turned on to allow all incoming calls to ring in the recreation center. When the attendant is away from the control counter, another switch activates a bell in the gym so that incoming calls can be heard from anywhere in the building. The phone company will be able to advise you further in this regard.

Locks and Keys: A system of locks and keys that takes into consideration which areas various persons should have access to will greatly facilitate control. The following system is suggested:

Outside: This should not be the same as that for the main church building, as you may have employees of the recreation facility who do not need access to the main church building.

Interior Rooms and Stairwells: The following should be keyed alike: stairwells, gymnasium, all-purpose room, game room, youth lounge, craft room, classrooms, locker rooms.

Interior offices, storage, etc.: The following should be keyed separately:

Equipment room
Secretary's office
Director's office
Kitchen
Kitchen pantry
Gym storage
All-purpose room storage
Craft room storage (workroom)
Other storage areas (inclusive)
Janitor's closets and mechanical areas

Mastering: Submasters should be made, as follows:

Sub-master A: All interior offices, storage, etc.
Sub-master B: All interior offices, storage, etc., except director's office
Sub-master C: Equipment room, gym storage, janitor's closets, and mechanical areas

Architect

One final word. Select an architect who has had experience in the design of recreation facilities. An experienced architect will be able to design the most functional building for the money.

8

LIMITED FACILITIES:
Making the Most of What You Have

Has your church hesitated to begin a recreation ministry because it doesn't have any facilities? Nonsense! On the contrary, most churches, even small ones, already have adequate facilities for a dynamic recreation ministry. The problem is they haven't discovered them. In this chapter, we'll help you do an inventory of your existing facilities and show you how, with a little ingenuity, they can be put to use in exciting ways. Also, we'll suggest that you look around the neighborhood and see what facilities may be available for the asking.

Inventory of Existing Facilities

Most churches are not aware of the potential that their present facilities offer for recreational programming. An inventory of existing facilities will often turn up a wealth of space that sits idle most of the time that could be put to use for a recreation ministry with little or no modification. So, the first step is an assessment of what you already have. Let's begin with a walking tour of your building. Where you start isn't important. You just want to be sure you cover all the space you have. Before you begin, you'll need two things: a number of copies of the "Inventory of Facilities: Rooms" form and a tape measure.

ROOMS

If your church is like most, it consists of a number of different rooms: Sunday school classrooms, conference rooms, reception areas, perhaps a fellowship hall, kitchen, chapel, maybe a youth lounge. Whatever the case, let's look carefully at each.

Size: Start with the first room you come to. What size is it? Measure the length and width to the nearest foot and multiply them together. If you get around 400 square feet, you have a small room; 800 or so, medium; 1200, large; 2400 or more, extra large.

Size will be a primary consideration in programming possibilities. A small room will accommodate up to twenty persons in a lecture format in which the participants are simply sitting and listening. If they will need tables to work on, particularly when they have to spread out materials, as in a water color class, the limit may be ten to twelve.

A medium room will permit people to spread out and have some space between them. A small bridge class, with six to eight tables can be handled in a medium-sized room. In addition, a medium-sized room will permit some movement in a small class such as yoga or exercise.

A large room can be used for active groups, such as ballet, exercise, or children's tumbling. Such a room will also accommodate table games, such as ping-pong, bumper pool, etc.

If you happen to have an extra large room, a number of recreation opportunities open up. Depending on ceiling height and floor surface (to be discussed later), you can conduct large exercise classes, have square dancing and rollerskating, do tumbling and gymnastics, play badminton, volleyball, or even basketball.

Shape: What's the shape of the room? Square? Rectangular? Odd shaped? Shape will dictate use to some extent. Make a note on the inventory form.

Floor Surface: Of what does the floor consist? Carpet is ideal for exercise classes; it is not ideal for ballet, rollerskating, or square dancing. Also, you will probably want a tile floor in a room housing an art class, where paint or other material is likely to be spilled.

INVENTORY OF FACILITIES: ROOMS

Room (name or #) _____

    Size: length _____ X width _____ = area _____ sq. ft.

           small (400) ___, medium (800) ___,

           large (1200) ____, extra large (2400) ____

    Shape: square ___, rectangular ___, other _____

    Floor Surface: tile ___, carpet ___, other _____

    Celing Height: _____ feet

    Ceiling Construction: _____

    Light Fixtures: flush ___, hanging ___

    Construction and Furnishing: _____

    _____

    Soundproofing: good ___, fair ___, poor ___

    Storage Areas: adjacent ___, near ___, none ___

    Special Equipment: _____

    Set Up: _____

    Primary Use: _____

    When Available: _____

    _____

    Possible Uses: _____

    _____

    _____

    Will any modification be necessary? _____ If so, what? _____

    _____

Ceiling Height: Ceiling height is not important in small- and medium-sized rooms, but a high ceiling in large and particularly in extra large rooms greatly increases the use possibilities. A ceiling height of 20' or more will enable you to play volleyball and basketball, as well as children's games involving a ball.

Ceiling Construction: Again, this is not important in small and medium rooms, but it is paramount if ball playing activities are to be done. The ultimate question is: will the ceiling be damaged by being struck by balls? Is it solid enough to withstand the impact of a volleyball or basketball, or will it be jarred loose or broken when it is hit?

Light Fixtures: What kind of light fixtures does the room have? Are they flush with the ceiling or are they hanging and fragile? Can hanging fixtures be replaced with flush ones?

Construction and Furnishing: What is the construction of the room? Is it made of durable concrete blocks that will withstand use and abuse, or is it of fragile construction and too finely furnished for recreational activities. Again, small rooms and medium rooms are not likely to receive the rough treatment that might occur in larger rooms where "play" takes place.

Soundproofing: How soundproof is the room? You might want to test it with a radio or tape player. Could, for instance, a phonograph be played in the room, say, for an exercise class, and not interfere with activities in adjacent rooms or those down the hall? While no room is completely soundproof, this factor will determine the things for which a room can be used.

Storage Areas: Are there adequate storage areas adjacent to or close by this room? If equipment, such as tumbling mats or gymnastic apparatus, will be used, there'll have to be a place to store it when it isn't being used.

Special Equipment: Does this room have any special equipment that would make it particularly appropriate for certain activities? Does it contain a sink which might be used to clean up from water color classes or ceramics of flower arranging? Does it have blackboards, cabinets for storing small items, such as greenware and glazes used in ceramics? Does it have a stage that would make dramatic activities possible?

Set Up: How is the room usually set up? Chairs in auditorium fashion, chairs around tables? Can chairs and tables be rearranged, or completely cleared out?

Primary Use: How is the room now being used? Is it used as a Sunday school classroom, a conference room, a Boy Scout Troop meeting room? Are there things on the walls and furnishings that need to remain in place? Would conducting a recreation activity in this room adversely affect its primary use?

When Available: When could this room be used for recreational purposes? Is it available on weekday mornings, afternoons, evenings? What about Saturdays?

Possible Uses: Before you leave the room, list several activities that this room could be used for. You may not even plan to have these activities, but the exercise of doing this will open up creative possibilities. Use your imagination. Is any modification necessary before it can be used? If so, what? Replace lights? Remove carpet? Now, go on to the next room and continue this process until all rooms have been inventoried.

PARKING LOT

Now let's go outside. Have you ever considered that a parking lot can be used for something other than parking cars? It can make a great volleyball court, a place to play badminton or even basketball. What's your parking lot like?

Size, Shape, Contour, Surface: We're not concerned here with the entire parking lot, but whether there is sufficient area for a volleyball court, for instance. The question is, do you have a flat, rectangular, smooth-surfaced area that is large enough for recreation activities. For volleyball, you'll need an unobstructed, rectangular area approximately 40' by 70' (the court area itself is 30' × 60'). The dimensions of various play and court areas are included in the last chapter. In the final analysis, are there one or more areas where athletic courts could be laid out?

Court Lines: Would it be possible to mark court lines on the parking lot without interfering with parking?

When Could It Be Used? Are there times when the area(s) under consideration is not needed for parking vehicles? What are those times?

Will Activities Disrupt the Flow of Traffic? Can the area be roped off and traffic routed around it? Will there be any danger in playing in that area?

Is It Lighted? With daylight savings time in effect, there will be times when you can use the area at night without lights. Lights, on the other hand, will give you greater versatility in programming. If there is lighting

INVENTORY OF FACILITIES: PARKING LOT
(Use a separate form for each area)

Size: length ___ X width ___

Shape: _____ (Draw a sketch)

Contour: Is the area flat enough to play on? ___

Surface: paved ___, dirt ___, grass ___, gravel ___

Court Lines: Can court markings be laid out without interfering
   with parking? ____

When Could It Be Used:

   Weekday mornings ___,   Weekday afternoons ___,
   Weekday evenings ___,   Saturday (times) _____
   Other (times) _____

Will It Disrupt Flow of Traffic When Used for Recreation? _____

   Can it be roped off during use? ___

   Is there any danger in using it? ___

Is It Lighted? ___

   Is lighting adequate for ball games? ____

   Can additional lights be added? ____

Possible Uses:

   Volleyball (30' X 60') ___

   Half-court Basketball (42' X 37') ____

   Full court Basketball (42' X 74') Junior High ____
                         (50' X 84') High School ____

   Badminton (20' X 44') ____

   Shuffleboard (6' X 52') _____

   Other _____

Note: Dimensions do not include sideline space.

already, is it sufficient for volleyball or basketball? You may want to go out one night and see. Can additional lights be added?

For What Can It Be Used? What are the programming possibilities? Volleyball? Basketball? (Half-court or full-court?) Badminton? One-wall racquetball (if there's an adjacent smooth-surfaced wall)? Here's where your ingenuity comes into play.

For years before we built our Family Center, our youth fellowship played volleyball on two courts on our parking lot every Wednesday night of the summer. In fact, even though we have a fine gymnasium, for tradition's sake, they continue to play outside even now. Recreation under the stars will always be appealing.

GRASSY AREAS, FIELDS, AND WOODS

After surveying your parking lot, the next step is to look around at any undeveloped property to see if it lends itself to recreational use. You may have a grassy area, an open field, a patch of woods. All have recreation potential and should be considered.

On the "Inventory of Facilities: Land" form are the dimensional requirements for various fields and playing areas. See if your land is suitable (with or without grading, clearing, cleaning, etc.) for activities such as softball, soccer, volleyball, horseshoes, croquet.

Size, Shape, Topography: The size, shape, and topography will dictate what can be done as far as playing fields are concerned. A grassy area may be perfect for croquet, volleyball, or horseshoes. An open field may be converted into a softball or soccer field. A wooded area may make an ideal picnic or day camp area. If there is a stream on the property, it too, has recreational possibilities. Use the accompanying form to assess your property's potential. After doing so, you may want to consult a landscape architect who can advise you on preparing the area(s).

Survey of Community Facilities

After you've discovered the facilities of your church that can be used for recreation, you might want to look around your neighborhood. There are probably facilities in your area that can be used by your church for your recreation ministry.

YMCAs and Other Organizations: Many YMCAs have gymnasiums that may be available. While gyms are in great demand, there may be some "non-prime" times when gyms can be used.

Schools: Both public and private schools sometimes have gymnasiums and/or playing fields. High school fields may be available during the summer for a softball league. Elementary schools may have playgrounds that can be used after school hours.

Parks: The local parks department may have fields available. You may find that there's a waiting list, but it'll be worth the wait if a field becomes available.

Private Land: Is there a piece of undeveloped land that is sitting in your neighborhood? Inquire into the possibility of using it on a temporary basis.

These suggestions are not far-fetched. On the contrary, what we've done may convince you to pursue the possibilities of using facilities in your community.

For many years our church had entered two softball teams in a church league in our community. The league policy stipulated that players had to be members or active participants of the church programs for which they played. In fact, when the roster was submitted to the league director at the beginning of the season, a minister had to certify that each player was, indeed, either a member or active participant in one of the programs of the church.

We felt it would be good for those who were not members of our church to play, since through recreation, they might become interested in the other programs of the church, but under the existing rules, that was forbidden. Therefore, we decided that if we could locate a playing field that we could use, we would form a league of our own and invite everyone to play — churched or unchurched. There was a playground in front of an elementary school in our neighborhood, so we approached the principal with our proposal: an adult softball league for both men and women — which would be open to anyone in the community.

The principal indicated that the field was already in use in the afternoons and on weekends for youth baseball practice. I noted that there were lights on the field and asked if they worked. He said that they had not been used in the time that he had been principal there. When we opened the switch box and turned them on, only three burned, one of which burned out while we were talking.

I asked him if we could use the field at night if we would replace the broken fixtures and repair the circuits. He indicated that he would have to have formal permission from the board of education, and that he would be willing to go to bat for us. Within a short time, we had obtained a permit to use the field on weeknights.

INVENTORY OF FACILITIES: LAND

(Use a separate form for each area)

Area: grassy ___, open field ____, woods ____, other _____

What possibilities do you see for this area?

   Softball ___ (Approximately 225' will be needed down the right
      and left field foul lines for adults.)

   Soccer ___ (55 yards X 100 yards to 65 yards X 110 yards)

   Volleyball ___ (30' X 60')

   Croquet court   (30' X 60')

   Horseshoes ___ (10' X 50')

   Picnic Area ___

   Day Camp Area ___

If you have a topographical map of your property, it would be a good
idea to lay out several play areas to see what you come up with. Where
there is land, there is the possibility for recreational use.

As we now had a place to play, we promoted our soft-ball program in the community and were able to orga-nize twelve teams. With some of the money from the registration fees, we repaired the lights. In addition, we did a number of things to the field that not only made it better for our purposes, it enhanced its usefulness for the students at the school. We added dirt to the infield area and improved drainage, we installed a new home plate and pitching rubber, put a chain across the en-trance to keep automobiles off, added benches which we left for the students to use, filled in holes in the outfield area and planted grass. While all of these improvements obviously were helpful to us, they also made for a better playground for the school. The PTA was so impressed with our stewardship of the field that they recommended our continued use.

As the school was now getting more requests than ever to use the field, because of its improvements, I sug-gested that the church take on the responsibility of scheduling its afterschool use. As a result, we were given authority to use the field during all afterschool hours, including weekends, provided that we schedule its use among other organizations wanting to use it in a fair and equitable manner. Our willingness to take on this responsibility, relieved the school of a burden that it did not want, and, at the same time, increased the com-munity use of the field.

This approach worked out so well that the next year the board of education granted us a five year lease on the field, with the option to renew the lease when it expires. Consequently, we were able to reach one of the long-range goals of our recreation ministry — the acquiring of a playing field on which to conduct our softball program. "We don't have any facilities" is a feeble excuse for not having a recreation ministry in your church. With the existing facilities and those available in your commu-nity, you can have a significant recreation ministry in your church. In fact, it's a good idea to begin a recrea-tion program *before* you build a facility. That way you will have time to determine exactly what you really need and want in the way of facilities. We played volleyball in our fellowship hall before we had a gymnasium in which to play. It was the use of those existing facilities that demonstrated the need for a recreation facility at our church.

9

OPERATION:
Using Your Facilities to Their Fullest

Before your facilities are completed and ready to move into, there are some basic decisions you will have to make in regard to its operation. In this chapter, we'll discuss your building's operation from the standpoints of *rules and policies, scheduling,* and *maintenance.*

Rules and Policies

In this section, our method will be to raise questions for consideration by you and your recreation committee. We'll also suggest answers that have worked for us. You may choose to do things differently, but you will have had some help in your "thinking through" process as you seek to determine your own rules and policies for operation.

1. Who will have access to your building?

Will your building be open to members only, or will you permit anyone to use your building? Will participation privileges be extended to those who are not "members" but attend church functions, such as worship services, Sunday school, etc.? In other words, will they have to "belong" to your church?

Whereas we have chosen to make our *programs* available to anyone in the community, we have also chosen to limit the *use* of our building (generally meaning the gymnasium during "open" periods) to only the members and those registered in our programs.

2. How will you control the use of your facilities?

Some churches issue each eligible person a name tag which is kept on file in the building. Those using the building are required to pick up their name tag upon entering. They must then wear the tag while in the facility, turning it back in when they leave. Name tags are helpful in enabling people to get to know one another, they provide a means of keeping up with who uses the facilities (the attendant checks off on a master list when the tags are returned to the file), and they provide control in that it will be easy to spot anyone in the building who does not have on a name tag. Some tags contain a pull-out insert which is left at the control counter when checking out equipment. (For more information on name tags and their use, contact the First Baptist Church, Tulsa, Oklahoma 74103.)

We have found that we can adequately control our building's use with "activity cards" which are shown to the control counter attendant when entering the building. A card is given to each member of our church who has completed the third grade. We do not require persons entering the building for a scheduled class or activity for which they are enrolled (since many of them are not members) to show a card.

Our activity card is wallet size. It has the seal of the church on it. We type the member's name on it, then laminate it in a machine that we purchased. By having our own laminating machine, we can easily prepare cards for new members. The card is then sent to each member, along with our information sheet, "Facilities, Policies, & Programs," (see sample in this chapter) on the use of the building.

Our activity cards are left with the control counter attendant when checking out equipment. They are returned to the member when the equipment is brought back.

You may decide to make activity cards (or name tags, or whatever) available to non-members. We did this for a while on a limited basis until our building use increased to the extent that we discontinued this policy. Whereas members' activity cards are permanent, we issued dated cards (of a different color to distinguish them from members') to non-members. The cards had to be renewed annually. We charged a small fee to non-members to help defray costs.

3. Will children be permitted to use the building?

Will you allow children to roam around in the building? Will they be limited to certain areas and to certain times? Our policy provides that children who have not yet completed the third grade have to be accompanied by a parent or guardian, or be part of an organized activity. Also, as we have a youth lounge for high school age members, we do not permit younger children in that area. Nor do we permit them on the second floor where there is minimum supervision.

4. Will you have a guest policy?

Will members be permitted to bring visitors with them? Most churches permit this, provided that members are with their guest and remain in the building while the guests are there. Some churches ask that guests fill out a visitor's card. Those churches using name tags have a special name tag for visitors. (Name tags for visitors may encourage members to introduce themselves and welcome visitors to the church.)

5. What hours will your building be open?

At what time will your building open each morning? What time will it close at night? Will you post a schedule of operating hours, and will it be visible from the outside of the building, in case someone comes by when the building is closed?

We generally open our offices at 8:30 A.M. on weekdays. Classes usually begin around 9:00 A.M. Closing time is dictated by the activities going on at night. Basketball, volleyball, and such are often not over until 10:30 or 11:00 P.M. We usually open on Saturday afternoons for drop-in basketball during the fall and spring. During the winter, our youth basketball leagues take up the gym until around 3:30 P.M. on Saturdays. We do not normally open the gym on Sundays except in the evenings for Youth Fellowship.

As activities change with the season, it is important to keep members apprised of changes in "open" periods when they can use the gym. Notices in the church bulletin and on the gym bulletin board will serve this function.

6. Will you have refreshments in your building?

Will you have vending machines in your building? Will they dispense soft drinks (in cans, bottles, or paper cups), or will they provide healthier beverages? What about candy, cookies, potato chips, etc.? Will consumption be limited to a "snack area" only, or will they be permitted in other parts of the building?

We dispense only soft drinks in cans (we feel they are less likely to get spilled, although some do) and while we do permit them to be taken into classrooms, we do not allow them in the gym. We turn off our drink machines at certain times, such as during Sunday school.

7. What about lockers?

Will you provide lockers? We do, and we permit members to put their personal locks on them, provided they remove the lock and contents when they leave the building. Lockers are particularly helpful for men and women who may be coming to use your facilities directly from work, in which case they need a place to store their dress clothes.

8. Will you have a "dress code?"

Some churches have requirements for dress in the gymnasium. We insist that gym shoes be worn (no black-soled jogging shoes which mar the floor). We do permit men and boys to play "shirts" and "skins" basketball, and simply ask that dress be "appropriate."

9. How are valuables handled?

If valuables are not locked in a locker, we encourage that they be checked-in at the control counter. We assume no responsibility for the loss of personal items which are not checked-in.

10. How will you handle "lost and found?"

You can count on clothing and other personal items being forgotten and left in your building. You can also count on people wanting to know where to look for them when they remember they have forgotten them. You will need to designate a place where they can be placed, and have a system for getting rid of items left over a certain period. A safety pin and a dated index card will accomplish this. After a period of thirty days, we give those items that are still unclaimed to organizations for the needy.

11. Will you permit smoking in you building?

We do not. If you don't you will need to post signs stating your policy.

PEACHTREE PRESBYTERIAN CHURCH FAMILY CENTER

LOCK-IN REQUEST

We are delighted to learn that your youth group will be using the Family Center in the near future. Our Family Center is equipped with a large gymnasium, game room, several meeting rooms, and shower facilities.

During your stay, one of our staff persons will be with you to assist you in any way possible.

Please fill out this form and return it to me as soon as possible so that we can prepare for your arrival.

- -

CHURCH_____

ADDRESS_____CITY_____STATE_____ZIP_____

PERSON IN CHARGE _____

POSITION _____HOME PHONE_____OFFICE PHONE_____

WHEN WILL YOU ARRIVE? Day _____Date_____Time_____

WHEN WILL YOU DEPART? Day _____Date_____Time_____

NUMBER OF PERSONS IN GROUP? _____boys _____girls. Av. Age _____

HOW MANY ADULT CHAPERONES _____

In requesting the use of the facilities of the Family Center I understand that the church named above is responsible for any damage or loss incurred to the building, facilities, or equipment as a result of our use. I also understand that we will be charged for cleaning the building if it is not left in the condition in which it is found.

SIGNED _____

PRINT NAME _____ TITLE _____

Our charge to cover the cost of a staff person and cleaning is $1.50 per person per night ($25.00 minimum). A deposit of $25.00 should be returned with this request. The balance will be due upon arrival.

Bill Maness, Recreation Director, Peachtree Presbyterian Church
3434 Roswell Road, N.W., Atlanta, GA   30363 (404-261-7651)

12. Will you have a policy on discipline?

Christian conduct is expected of all persons who use our facilities. Some churches have a discipline and suspension policy that provides for: warning on the first infraction, a one-day suspension and call to parents (if a child) for the second, a longer suspension and conference with the violator (and parents) for the third.

13. How will you handle injuries?

In spite of every precaution, active people will sometimes be injured. During an adult basketball season, you can expect twisted knees, sprained ankles, dislocated fingers, concussions. Our control counter attendants are trained in first aid, and we keep a well-stocked first-aid kit. In addition, we keep a ready supply of ice (since we have a refrigerator with an ice maker) and plastic bags for cold packs. An accident report should be made on any serious injury, recording the name of victim, address, phone, what the injury was and how it occured, how it was treated, the time of occurrence, and the names of those who were witnesses, as well as the name of the one making the report.

14. Will you have accident insurance?

While we have accident insurance that will cover someone if they fall down the steps or get hit by a door, we do not have coverage for injuries resulting from participating in any athletic endeavor, whether it be roller-skating, a basketball or softball game or practice, or a pick-up volleyball game. The cost of such insurance makes it prohibitive, and we have found that most individuals carry accident insurance of their own. It is important, however, that you notify you participants of your policy so there won't be any misunderstanding when injuries occur.

15. What groups inside and outside of the church will be permitted to use the recreation facilities?

We encourage Sunday school and other church-related groups to reserve the Family Center for parties and special activities. Saturday nights are set aside for such groups, but other times are also available when scheduling permits. Some churches, ours included, limit use to church sponsored groups. While we do not charge for use, we do insist that the building be left in the condition in which it was found.

We also honor requests from other churches with youth groups for "lock-in" arrangements where they can spend the night while on tour. We charge for this service in order to pay one of our staff to stay with groups overnight. A sample of our lock-in request form is included here.

16. Who is responsible for lost or damaged equipment?

Usually, equipment that is lost or damaged is the responsibility of the individual or group that was using it. You may want to provide for such in your policy statement.

In conclusion, remember, as you sit down to formulate your set of rules and policies that your recreation ministry can become encumbered with undue attention to restrictive regulations. I've seen multi-paged booklets outlining in infinite detail sets of rules for the operation of a building. Rules are meant to facilitate the operation, not cripple it with minutiae. The Pharisees were severely criticized for "tithing mint and cumin and neglecting the weightier matters of the law." The weightier matters in this case are the "renewing of the spirit and making glad the heart" mentioned earlier. Policies that are rigid and inflexible can stifle the enjoyment and freedom of expression that should come from the use of your building.

We even go one step further. We will often "overlook" our rules when overlooking makes for a smoother operation. You'll see a number of rules and regulations that we do not adhere to unless it is necessary. We have not checked an activity card in years; we frequently have members of the community drop in during open periods and we welcome them and do everything we can to see that they enjoy themselves.

There are occasions, however, when you will need to enforce rules, and you should have them in written form for those occasions you will need them. Such an occasion occured not long ago in our building. For years we have played pick-up co-ed volleyball every Tuesday night. We have placed no restrictions on who participated, and often non-members come by and play. On one occasion, however, a volleyball "team" from another organization found that we had an *open* policy and decided to use our gym as a place to hold its practice. We asked them not to come again as we felt they were not participating in the spirit in which our volleyball night had been set up.

Listed below are our rules and policies. We thought it might serve as a guide in your preparation of one for your church. Notice that ours contains a brief description of our *facilities,* a listing of the *program areas* in our recreation ministry, as well as mentioning our *brochure,* the *need to register* for classes, and our *fee policy.* This information is included in our "new member packet" given to those who join the church.

FACILITIES, POLICIES, & PROGRAMS

FACILITIES

Let's begin by looking at the Family Center itself. The focal point of the main floor is the multi-purpose Gymnasium. It contains a regulation NCAA basketball court as well as two smaller cross courts. The height of the goals on the cross courts is adjustable to accommodate youth games. In addition, the gym floor is lined for volleyball and one-wall handball. The gym features a "floating" floor which is particularly comfortable to play on.

Just outside the gym, toward the front of the building is the Game Room, equipped for ping-pong, pool, and other table games. Next to the game room is the Arts & Crafts Room with a kiln for firing pottery and ceramic pieces.

Across the lobby is the Control Counter. An attendant will be on duty there during all open periods to assist you.

The main floor also contains restrooms and locker and shower facilities which may be entered either from the lobby or from the gymnasium.

The second floor contains the Great Room, Youth Lounge, a Kitchen, and three Classrooms. The recreation director's office is also located on the second floor.

POLICIES

Activity Cards: Each member of Peachtree Presbyterian Church (including their children) will be given a Family Center Activity Card. This card should be shown to the control counter attendant when you enter the building (unless you are coming for a scheduled activity or class for which you have already enrolled). The Activity Card will also be used when checking out equipment, such as, basketballs, roller skates, etc.

Non-Members: Persons who are not members of Peachtree Presbyterian Church may purchase a Family Center Activity Card.

Guests: Church members may bring guests to the Family Center at any time by simply indicating to the control counter attendant who their guests are when showing their Activity Card.

Children: Children who have not yet completed the third grade must be accompanied by a parent or guardian, or be a part of an organized activity, when using the Family Center, the children who have not yet entered high school will not be allowed on the second floor, except for scheduled activities.

Hours of Operation: The Family Center will be open from 9:00 A.M. until 9:30 P.M. Monday through Friday, and from 12:00 noon until 5:00 P.M. on Saturdays. It may be open at other times for special activities. A listing of open times and regularly scheduled activities will be posted on the bulletin board in the lower lobby, however, they are subject to change as needed.

Refreshments: Vending machines are located in the concession area adjacent to the lower lobby. All refreshments must be consumed within the concession area.

Equipment: Recreation equipment may be checked out at the control counter by exchanging your Activity Card for the equipment desired. When the equipment is returned, your card will be returned. The cost of repair or replacement of damaged or lost equipment must be paid by the one to whom it was checked out.

Locker Rooms: Lockers are available for storing clothes only while using the facilities. Personal locks may be used but must be removed when you leave.

Valuables: Valuables may be checked in at the control counter. The church assumes no responsibility for loss of personal items which were not checked in.

Bulletin Boards: There are two bulletin boards in the Family Center. The one in the lower lobby will be used for posting notices concerning the operation of the Family Center. The one in the second floor lobby will be used by the young people of the church. No personal notices will be permitted on either board.

Lost & Found: Lost articles will be dated and kept at the control counter for a period of 30 days; if not claimed within that time, they will be given to organizations for the needy.

Towels: The church does not furnish towels.

Classes: Classes and special activities will have preferential use over open periods whenever there is a conflict.

Arts & Crafts Room: The Arts & Crafts Room is to be used only for scheduled classes and when an instructor is present.

Game Room: The game room may be used during all open periods. Ping-pong balls may be purchased at the control center.

Accidents: In spite of every possible precaution, active people will sometimes be injured. The control counter attendant is trained in first aid and any injury should be brought to his or her attention.

Reservations: Church related groups are encouraged to reserve the Family Center for parties and special activities. Saturday nights are set aside for such groups, but other times can be made available. Contact the recreation director for more information.

Conduct: Christian action and conduct are expected of all persons using the Family Center. Smoking is not permitted in the building.

PROGRAMS

The Recreation program at Peachtree is divided into four major areas:

Youth: Youth activities are held throughout the school year in the afternoons. During the summer, special week-long programs are planned.

Fitness: A variety of exercise programs are offered for men and women both in the mornings and evenings. In addition, weight reducing classes and classes on "how to exercise" are conducted regularly.

Arts, Crafts, & Hobbies: A diverse and exciting array of classes is offered throughout the year, including such regulars as: ballet, modern jazz, ceramics, painting, decoupage, home decorating, etc. In addition, new and different classes appear each quarter.

Sports: A full and varied sports program is conducted on a seasonal basis for all ages. Complete details are made available along with ample time for registration.

"Recreation at Peachtree": A quarterly brochure, "Recreation at Peachtree," which describes the classes and activities in the aforementioned areas, is mailed to each member's household. In addition, special announcements are sent out from time to time, and regular announcements and reminders pertaining to recreation appear in the weekly bulletin.

Registration: So that we can serve you in the most efficient way, it is necessary to register in advance for all classes and special activities. Registration instructions always accompany information on classes.

Fees: The fees charged for the various classes and activities cover the direct costs involved. Fees will be refunded if you withdraw from a class or activity prior to its first meeting.

Scheduling

A day or so before your classes are set to begin, you will need to prepare a schedule of those classes and activities you will be having. It would be nice to be able to do this earlier, but I have found that many people wait to the last minute to sign up for classes (despite our efforts to encourage them to register early). As a result, you may not know until a day or so before they are scheduled to begin which classes will "make it" and which will have to be cancelled due to insufficient enrollment. In addition, because people are often slow to register, you will not know until the last moment how many will be in each class so you can detemine the appropriate classroom size.

Therefore, at some time close to your starting date, a schedule will have to be made. When classes are to begin on a Monday, my secretary and I usually perform this task on the preceding Thursday. Using a form similar to the one shown on the next page, we block out the morning, afternoon, and evening classes for each day of

DAY _____	MORNING	AFTERNOON	EVENING
GYM			
GAME			
CRAFT			
GREAT			
201			
202			
203			

the week. The decision as to where each class will meet is based on its requirements. For example, ballet needs a large room with a hard floor, so it is put in our Great Room. Yoga, having eighteen enrolled and needing a "soft" surface to exercise on is put in our medium-sized, carpeted Game Room. The same procedure is followed for each class for each day.

When this process is completed, a master schedule (see sample) is prepared. The master schedule contains not only the room assignment and meeting time, but also the instructor's name and the setup and equipment needed. A copy of this master schedule is then given to those persons responsible for seeing that the rooms are set up properly, namely the janitor and the control counter attendant.

The janitor follows the schedule for setting up rooms, being sure that setups for evening classes are made before going off duty. The control counter attendant who comes on duty each evening then double checks to see that each room is ready for the class.

In addition, we make an enlarged copy of the master schedule (without the setups) and post it on our bulletin board. (Most print shops can make enlargements of typewritten material which makes attractive copy for bulletin boards.)

FAMILY CENTER CLEANING SCHEDULE

Area	2×/day	Daily	2×/week	Weekly	As needed
Gymnasium	Mop/scrape for gum	Setups: V-ball net(s) P.L.A.Y. equip., etc.	Vacuum inter- section of floor & walls	Clean backboards	Replace nets & lights
Storage rooms				Clean & straighten	
Men's & women's locker rooms	Clean sinks Check toilet paper & towels	Hose &/or mop floors Clean toilets Clean mirrors		Dust lockers	
Concession area		Mop & clean furniture	Restock machine		
Lower lobby		Vacuum carpet Clean counter	Clean glass		
Secretary's office			Vacuum		
Equipment room				Mop floor	
Craft room		Setup for classes	Mop floor		Setup for classes
Game room		Setup for classes	Vacuum carpet Clean tables		
Entrances			Sweep		
Sidewalks				Sweep	
Stairs		Mop &/or sweep			
Upper lobby & hall			Mop &/or sweep		
Upstairs restrooms		Clean Check toilet paper & towels			
201,202,203		Setup for classes	Clean		
Great room		Mop &/or sweep Setup for classes			
Youth room		Setup for classes	Vacuum carpet Dust furniture		
Kitchen			Mop Clean counters, etc.		
Director's office			Vacuum		
General		Empty trash cans		Clean glass	Change AC filters Replace lights

RECREATION ACTIVITIES SCHEDULE

Winter - 1980

Time	Class & Instructor	Room	Equipment

MONDAY

Time	Class & Instructor	Room	Equipment
8:50 am	Ladies Exer.(Simmons)	Gym	Mats, phono
9:00 am	Bridge (Strickland)	Great Rm	10 Tbl.,b'bd.
9:15 am	Ladies Exer.(Simmons)	Gym	/40 chairs
10:15 am	Ladies Exer.(Simmons)	Gym	
10:30 am	Bridge (Strickland)	Great Rm	
1:30 pm	Arbor Academy	Gym	
3:30 pm	"Be-a-Sport" (Straus)	Gym	Nerf balls
4:30 pm	7&8 Boys B'ball	gym	8½' baskets
5:45 pm	8-10,11&12 Girls B'ball	gym	(2) 8½; (2) 9'
6:00 pm	Ladies Ex. (McCamish)	F'ship Hall	mats, phono
7:00 pm	Bridge (Strickland)	Youth Lng.	8 Tbl,32 chrs.
7:00 pm	Boy Scouts	Great Rm	
7:00 pm	Ladies Ex. (McCamish)	F'ship Hall	
7:15 pm	Ladies B'ball League	Gym	60 chr, table
8:00 pm	Yoga (Stevens)	Ptree Rm.	

TUESDAY

Time	Class & Instructor	Room	Equipment
9:30 am	Flower Arr. (Swink)	Craft Rm.	Proj, screen
1:30 pm	Arbor Academy	Gym	
1:30 pm	Bridge (Strickland)	Great Rm	10 tbls, 40 ch.
3:30 pm	"Be-a-Sport" (Straus)	Gym	Nerf balls
4:30 pm	9&10 Boys B'ball	Gym	9' baskets
5:45 pm	9&10,11&12 Boys B'ball	Gym	(2) 9'; (2), 10'
7:00 pm	Bridge (Strickland)	Great Rm	
7:30 pm	S.A.T. (Finsthwait)	Game Rm	36 chrs, b'board
7:30 pm	Guitar (Oliver)	Youth Lng.	12 chrs, b'board
7:30 pm	Ceramics (Rainer)	Craft Rm	
7:30 pm	Calligraphy (Rogers)	Room 201	
8:00 pm	Volleyball	Gym	Both nets
8:00 pm	Square Dancing (Worley)	F'ship Hall	
8:30 pm	Bridge (Strickland)	Great Rm	

Maintenance

Your maintenance program will revolve around the schedule we have just discussed. To a great extent, the working agenda of your janitor will depend on your class schedule. Room setups, because they must be completed by a certain time, will take priority over everything else. Your janitor will spend endless hours each week putting up and taking down tables and chairs. Chairs and tables will have to be set up for bridge and taken down for ballet. Movie projectors and phonographs will be moved from storage closet to rooms and back to storage closet time after time.

In addition, the janitor will have to find time in between to vacuum carpets, sweep the gym floor, empty trash cans, keep soap and paper in the dispensers, restock the drink machine, mop the locker room floor, clean blackboards, wash windows, etc. The janitor will have to do this in a building that will be used seven days a week, week-in-week-out, and in a building that will receive at best "rough" treatment. He can count on having drinks spilled on carpets, chewing gum stuck to the gym floor, ceiling panels broken by balls, despite your best efforts to control this.

What we have found to be helpful is a flexible schedule of cleaning similar to the one shown on the preceding page. Rather than preparing a day-by-day list of things to do, we have, instead, outlined those areas that need regular attention: some twice a day, some once a day; some twice a week, some weekly. A day-by-day list, because our building schedule changes frequently, would necessitate constant revising. This more flexible one has worked well for us.

There will also be those things in the area of maintenance that will need attention by a staff maintenance person or by some outside repair service. Phonographs will break, faucets will leak, door handles will come off, light switches will quit working. There needs to be some mechanism for getting prompt attention. We have found a "Work Request Card" helpful. The sample shows who

```
┌─────────────────────────────────┐
│                                 │
│   W O R K    R E Q U E S T      │
│                                 │
│ Requested by_____ │
│                                 │
│ Date_____ Needed by_____ │
│                                 │
│ Job Request_____ │
│                                 │
│ _____  │
│                                 │
│ _____  │
│                                 │
│ Location_____ │
│                                 │
│ _____  │
│                                 │
│ Assigned to_____ │
│                                 │
│ Completed _____ on_____  │
│                                 │
│                                 │
└─────────────────────────────────┘
```

the work is requested by, when the request was made, when it needs to be completed, what needs attention, and where it is located. This is given to the building superintendant who assigns the work.

Remember, when you move into a new building, your work has just begun. It will require diligent attention to see that your facility is appropriately regulated, efficiently scheduled, and adequately maintained.

10

DIRECTION:
Implementing the Program

There are some things that should be said in regard to the person who will have the responsibility for the implementation of the recreation ministry and those individuals who will be partners in this ministry, the secretary and the recreation committee.

Recreation Director/Minister of Recreation

The single most important ingredient in the development and continuation of a successful recreation ministry is the director (or minister, as the case may be). The word that most aptly describes the role of this individual is "catalyst." A catalyst, by definition, "initiates a reaction and enables it to proceed under control." Your church has a mixture of many elements which have the potential for combining into a recreation ministry — facilities (perhaps), people (certainly), ideas, needs, interests, hopes. It is the reaction of these and other elements within your church that will result in your ministry of recreation. The recreation director is the one who will get the reaction going and keep it going and keep it under control.

In this section, we'll look at some qualifications and responsibilities of a recreation director, and some tips that I've learned from personal experience on getting the job done.

QUALIFICATIONS

Personal

A person being considered for the position of recreation director must, first of all, be a Christian. In addition, he or she must be dedicated to the proposition that recreation is, and ought to be, an integral part of a church's total ministry. He or she must believe in the role which recreation can play in furthering the mission of the church and in complementing the other activities of the church. (A church would do well to seek a person who senses a "calling" to the ministry and this type of work.)

Professional

The person wanting to be a recreation director in a church should be a college graduate (and preferably have a seminary degree) with training and/or experience in recreation and physical education. He or she should have a wide knowledge of individual and team sports and be enthusiastic about them. Athletic ability is helpful, but not essential. The individual should also be familiar with non-sports recreational activities.

RESPONSIBILITIES

Administrative: The recreation director is responsible for the administration of the recreation program including the hiring and supervision of full and part-time staff, operating a facility (including scheduling and maintenance of it), preparation and management of a budget, selection and purchase of equipment.

Recruiting and Training: The responsibilities include the recruiting and training of volunteer personnel such as coaches, officials, and those involved in non-sports activities.

Program: The recreation director must plan and implement a broad-based program, offering a variety of classes and activities that serve the needs and interests of all ages.

Peachtree Presbyterian Church
3434 ROSWELL ROAD, N.W.
ATLANTA, GA. 30363

Dear Coach:

The softball program at Peachtree has some exciting
possibilities for ministry, both to our members and to
many who do not belong to this, or perhaps any, church.

You'll be interested to know that 87 of the 165 persons
(52%) playing on our twelve teams are not members of this
church.

Consequently, I am writing a letter to every Peachtree
member on your team asking if they will contact one (in
some cases, two) teammates to invite them to come to
Sunday school or church. A copy of the letter is attached.
You may also receive one in the mail.

I am well aware that having as many non-members as we do
this year is not as "comfortable" a situation as it has
been in the past when we were, for the most part, all
home-folks. On the ohter hand, look at the opportunity
that we have to say to the community, "We love our church
and would like for you to be a part of it too."

I encourage you, as coach of your team, to remind your
players that our concern is not just winning games, but
enjoying Christian fellowship, making new friends, and
uplifting Christ in our actions and attitudes.

I am enclosing the following:

   1. A copy of the league rules and regulations
   2. Schedules for each of your players
   3. A supply of lineup cards

Thank you for taking on this responsibility.

Sincerely,

Bill Maness

M/p
Enclosures

Peachtree Presbyterian Church
3434 ROSWELL ROAD, N.W.
ATLANTA, GA. 30363

Dear _____*Greg*_____ :

    "Witnessing" is not necessarily standing up in church to be counted or preaching on street corners. Sometimes it is at its most effective when one person speaks directly to another, extending an invitation to share Christian experiences and services in church.

    Since you play on a softball team, you are no doubt aware that some members of your team do not belong to our church, or perhaps to any church. Would you be willing to ask *Tom Smith* to come to Sunday school, perhaps the *SCIONS* class, and attend church services soon? This might make a big difference in the life of your fellow player.

    I hope that you will help our church family to open new doors for others in our community.

Sincerely,

Bill

Bill Maness

Recreation Director

M/p

Promotion: The responsibility for developing and distributing publicity and for promoting the recreation ministry through personal appearances before Sunday school classes and other groups in the church will belong to the recreation director.

Integration: The director should work with the other ministers on the staff to see that the various ministries of the church complement one another and should function as a part of a ministerial team, working on committees and in projects, lending enthusiastic support to the total ministry of the church.

Nurture: The minister of recreation must be cognizant of the opportunities for nurture that are inherent in recreation. It should be a primary concern to see that "nurturing" takes place in the recreation experience of individuals.

Evangelism: Evangelism doesn't just happen. It is the result of an effort to make it happen.

One of the primary responsibilities of the director of recreation is to see that recreation is, indeed, a ministry. He or she should make it a point to see that all those who are not members of the church but participate in a recreation activity are contacted either personally or by phone or by letter, to insure that they are aware that recreation in the church is only part of a ministry to the total person.

In this regard, the director can call many of them. In addition, he or she can facilitate the personal contact by team members and classmates by a simple note to those members who are participating, reminding them that many are not members and suggesting that they invite them to church. Two samples of letters doing this are included.

TIPS

I want to include some tips ("secrets of success," if you will) that I've learned through experience that have been helpful to me. I'm passing them along for whatever they're worth:

Be a Promoter

You will be the most effective publicity there can be for your program. If you believe in what you're doing and are enthusiastic about it, others will recognize it and want to participate. I've had the most success when I go to Sunday school classes — both children's and adult's — and personally tell people about the programs and activities in our recreation ministry.

Delegate, but . . .

Your ministry will be limited unless you can learn to delegate responsibility to others. Remember, however, to delegate means to "entrust," it does not mean to "give." The responsibility remains *yours*.

Be Visible

A recreation director ought to be seen. I try to make it a point to be around at basketball practice, at softball games, and at other recreation activities. Your presence conveys your interest. In that regard, no one can take your place.

Participate

I've found it's not much fun to work while others are playing, therefore, I determined to enjoy being a recreation director by participating in the things that are going on. I play on a softball team, coach basketball, compete in golf tournaments. If you do so, you'll find it not only helps you, it'll make your ministry a better one too.

Pay Attention to Details

It's easy to concern yourself with the "big" things and assume the details will take care of themselves. They won't. It's attention to details that makes the difference between a mediocre and a good ministry.

Act Decisively

Early in my ministry I had to replace a basketball coach in mid-season. I felt it had to be done in order to maintain the integrity of our program. To tolerate the situation would have jeopardized everything we were striving for. Don't hesitate to make the difficult decisions when you are convinced that they are in the best interest of your ministry.

Recreation Secretary

The first impression that many will have of your recreation ministry is that which is conveyed by your recreation secretary. This person is the one with whom they will first talk when they call and with whom they will first deal when they drop by. In that regard, the secretary should, first of all, love people and should not only be tolerant of their idiosyncracies, but anxious to be helpful in spite of them. The secretary must be patient enough to answer a myriad of questions and interested enough to supply answers to those not asked and be cognizant of people's needs and respond accordingly.

The secretary must believe in the inherent role of

recreation in the church and be enthusiastic about it. (The recreation director, in this regard, has the responsibility of instructing the secretary as to the director's philosophy of recreation.)

The basic secretarial skills — typing, shorthand, some knowledge of bookkeeping — are needed, as well as a good command of the English language. The person should be a self-starter — one who looks for things that need to be done — and should be creative — looking for better ways to do things. The secretary should, last of all, be able to work under pressures, for the job will be filled with noise, repeated interruptions, and, from time to time, general madness.

Recreation Committee

A recreation committee should be formed to establish policy, provide council to the recreation director, and to oversee the implementation of the recreation ministry. A recreation committee should be comprised of officers of the church and members-at-large who represent the various elements of the congregation: youth, singles, young families, middle-aged persons, the elderly. In addition, various interests — sports, fitness, arts & crafts, youth activities — should have representation.

In the selection of a committee, it is important to look for members who not only represent particular interests or age groups, but have a broad concern for the overall program. It is possible to have members who have their "pet" projects and make little or no contribution to the ministry of recreation as a whole.

A rotating term of office in which one-third of the committee members is replaced every year gives continuity to the committee and, at the same time, allows new members to be added on a regular basis.

A recreation committee should meet monthly to review, evaluate, and plan programs. While the committee will have the responsibility of setting policy, adopting a budget, designing facilities, selecting equipment, setting fees, its primary role will be the assessing of the needs of the congregation and determining of ways to meet those needs.

11

POTPOURRI:
A Collection of "Bits & Pieces"

Some of the "little" things that do not fit neatly into any of the chapters, nor warrant a chapter unto themselves, are, nonetheless, worthy of discussion. The mere listing in an appendix would not do them justice. Therefore, this chapter is a presentation of those "bits & pieces" that are left over and should be included somewhere.

Recreation Workshops

Even a recreation director needs to be "renewed" from time to time. I have found that there is nothing to compare to the physical, mental, and spiritual renewal that can occur at a recreation workshop where directors and lay persons meet to learn new skills, share program ideas, and worship together. It is an experience that should have top priority in the schedule of a recreation director. In addition, key lay persons from your church should also be encouraged to attend.

Workshops generally offer a variety of practical "how-to" courses in such things as: games, crafts, family camping, puppet making and manipulation, square dance calling, clogging, clowning, story telling, drama, party planning, youth retreats, etc. The opportunity to meet and exchange ideas with others who are doing the same things you are is as valuable as the courses.

Listed below are workshops sponsored by three different denominations. Check with your denomination, if not listed, to see if it, too, has any workshops.

ANNUAL RECREATION WORKSHOP

"Patterns in Recreation" is sponsored by the Presbyterian Church in the United States. This week-long workshop is held annually in early May in Montreat, North Carolina. For information, write to: Annual Recreation Workshop, Presbyterian School of Christian Education, 1205 Palmyra Avenue, Richmond, Virginia 23227.

REC-LAB

The Southern Baptist Convention sponsors two one-week workshops each year in January: one in Lake Yale, Florida; the other in Glorieta, New Mexico. For details, write to: Rec-Lab, Church Recreation Department, Baptist Sunday School Board, 127 Ninth Avenue, North, Nashville, Tennessee 37234.

RECREATION WORKSHOP

The United Methodist Church conducts a week-long workshop in Gallant, Alabama each spring, usually the week after Easter. For information, write to: Recreation Workshop, Southeastern Jurisdictional Council on Ministries, 159 Ralph McGill Boulevard, N.E., Atlanta, Georgia 30365.

Puppets

I am convinced that puppets can offer one of the most exciting and challenging opportunities in a recreation ministry. Puppets are not only entertaining, they are unparalleled for their effectiveness in communication. With the help of puppets, a children's Sunday school class can take on new dimensions. To teach, one must have the attention of the pupil. Puppets can literally *capture* the minds of little children to the point where they are not only listening, they actually become *involved* in the lesson. I commend this alluring mode of communication to you. It can make Sunday school fun, and shouldn't it be?

Recreation Library

As soon as possible, you should begin to build a library of recreation books. I thought about including a bibliography, but have decided not to for two reasons: first, new books on the various aspects of recreation are being published so fast that a bibliography would be out of date by the time it is printed; second, I like to look through a book before I buy it. My suggestion, therefore, is to make periodic trips to your denominational and other bookstores and browse a bit. Your library will be most valuable as you begin to accumulate those books that will be available to those lay persons whom you've recruited to lead in recreation programs.

Nursery

A nursery is essential if you are going to have morning recreation classes. Mothers with pre-school children, and that will be a sizeable contingency, will likely not be able to participate unless a nursery is provided.

On our application form, we have a place to indicate whether a nursery is needed so that we will know how many children need to be cared for. Some churches require payment in advance for the entire session; others accept payment each time the child is brought.

Athletic Equipment

Athletic equipment is expensive. There is frequently the tendency to shop around for price. We made the mistake several years ago of purchasing volleyball standards and mounting plates of lesser quality because they sold for about half the price of top of the line equipment. After only a few uses, it was readily apparent that they lacked durability. Volleyball standards, as well as other equipment that has to be repeatedly set up and taken down, and is subjected to rugged use, should be of the highest quality affordable if you want it to give lasting service.

Wanting to prepare a list of athletic equipment manufacturers, I wrote to more than forty companies which produce sports equipment, stating that I was writing a book and wanted to consider including their product in it. The following list was compiled from those companies who chose to respond by sending a catalogue.

I have placed an asterisk (*) by the names of those manufacturers from whom I have either purchased equipment and/or seen it in use and have found it to be of high quality. The lack of an asterisk indicates only that I am not personally familiar with their equipment.

BASKETBALL BACKSTOPS

Medart, Incorporated*
P.O. Box 658
Greenwood, Mississippi 38930

Porter Equipment Company
955 Irving Park Road
Schiller Park, Illinois 61076

BLEACHERS (PORTABLE)

American Athletic Equipment (AMF)*
200 American Avenue
Jefferson, Iowa 50129

CERAMIC PRODUCTS

American Art Clay Company, Inc.
4717 West Sixteenth Street
Indianapolis, Indiana 46222

Skutt Ceramic Products*
2618 S.E. Steele Street
Portland, Oregon 97202

GYMNASTIC EQUIPMENT (INCLUDING MATS)

American Athletic Equipment (AMF)*
200 American Avenue
Jefferson, Iowa 50129

Nissen Corporation*
P.O. Box 1270
Cedar Rapids, Iowa 52406

Porter Equipment Company
955 Irving Park Road
Schiller Park, Illinois 60176

LOCKERS

Lyon Metal Products*
P.O. Box 671
Aurora, Illinois 60507

NAME TAGS

Discount Trophy and Engraving
4262 Cadiz
Fort Worth, Texas 76133

POOL TABLES

Brunswick Corporation
Consumer Division
Skokie, Illinois 60077

ROLLERSKATES

Chicago Rollerskate Company*
4450 West Lake Street
Chicago, Illinois 60624

RC Sports, Inc.
315 North Lindenwood
Olathe, Kansas 66061

SCOREBOARDS

Coca-Cola Company*
Check with the Coca-Cola Company in your area.
In many instances, they will supply, install, and
service a scoreboard at no cost if you sell their
products in your vending machines.

Fair-Play Scoreboards
P.O. Box 1847-S
Des Moines, Iowa 50306

Nevco Scoreboard Company
215-225 E. Harris Avenue
Greenville, Illinois 62246

TABLE GAMES

World Wide Games*
Box 450
Delaware, Ohio 43015

TABLE TENNIS TABLES

American Athletic Equipment (AMF)*
200 American Avenue
Jefferson, Iowa 50129

UNIFORMS

Champion Products*
3141 Monroe Avenue
Rochester, New York 14618

VOLLEYBALL EQUIPMENT

American Athletic Equipment (AMF)
200 American Avenue
Jefferson, Iowa 50129

Nissen Corporation*
P.O. Box 1270
Cedar Rapids, Iowa 52406

Porter Equipment Company
9555 Irving Park Road
Schiller Park, Illinois 60176

League and Tournament Scheduling

One of the recurrent functions of a recreation director will be the scheduling of league and tournament
competition.

We usually begin a season with round robin play so
that each team has a chance to play each of the other
teams at least one time, and we conclude with a tournament of one kind or another. A tournament at the end
helps maintain interest throughout the season, particularly for those teams that may not have a good record.

ROUND ROBIN SCHEDULING

In round robin play, each team is assigned a number
and pairings are determined by the number of teams in-

volved. (Note that with an odd number of teams, one
team has a bye (X) in each round.)

In case you have more than eight teams, there are
two formulas for determining pairings: one for an even
number and one for an odd number of teams.

4 Teams

2-1	4-2	4-1
3-4	1-3	2-3

5 Teams

1-4	3-1	5-3	2-5	4-2
2-3	4-5	1-2	3-4	5-1
5-X	2-X	4-X	1-X	3-X

6 Teams

2-1	3-4	6-4	5-3	5-6
4-5	6-1	2-3	6-2	1-3
3-6	2-5	1-5	4-1	4-2

7 Teams

1-6	4-2	2-7	5-3	3-1	6-4	7-5
2-5	5-1	3-6	6-2	4-7	7-3	1-4
3-4	6-7	4-5	7-1	5-6	1-2	2-3
7-X	3-X	1-X	4-X	2-X	5-X	6-X

8 Teams

5-6	3-4	7-8	7-5	1-3	3-6	8-2
3-8	1-7	6-2	6-1	4-2	4-5	7-3
4-7	8-6	4-1	2-3	5-8	2-7	1-5
2-1	2-5	5-3	8-4	6-7	8-1	6-4

FOR AN EVEN NUMBER OF TEAMS

Begin with No. 1 in the top left hand column and list the remaining numbers in a clockwise (down the right column and up
the left) fashion. With ten teams, for example, you would have:

1-2		1-10	1-9	1-8
10-3		9-2	8-10	7-9
9-4	then	8-3	7-2	6-10
8-5		7-4	6-3	5-2
7-6		6-5	5-4	4-3

Then, for the second and succeeding rounds, simply keep No.
1 stationary and rotate the other numbers one position clockwise for each round. Continue in this fashion until each round
has been formed.

FOR AN ODD NUMBER OF TEAMS

With an odd number of teams, begin with the highest
number in the top left column, place a bye (X) next to it, and
then list the remaining numbers in a clockwise (down the
right column and up the left) fashion. For example, with nine
teams, you would have:

9-X		8-X	7-X
8-1		7-9	6-8
7-2	then	6-1	5-9
6-3		5-2	4-1
5-4		4-3	3-2

TOURNAMENTS

A team's standing after round robin play is usually used to determine seeding in a tournament.

Single-Elimination

A single-elimination tournament is the quickest method of determining a winner. Whenever a team loses, it is eliminated from competition.

A typical bracket looks like this:

Note the pairings (seeding) are based on how a team finishes in round robin play.

Consolation Tournament

A consolation tournament enables each entry to play at least two games before being eliminated. The winner of the loser's side (B) may play the winner of the winner's side (G) for the championship, or team B may be declared the runner-up.

Here is an example of a consolation tournament bracket:

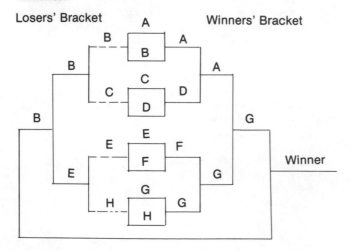

Double-Elimination Tournament

A double-elimination tournament, in which a team continues to play until it loses two times, requires much longer to play than either a single-elimination or a consolation tournament. Should the winner of the loser's bracket defeat the winner of the winner's bracket, the teams play a second game to decide the championship (when one team will have lost two games).

Brackets for a double-elimination tournament look like this:

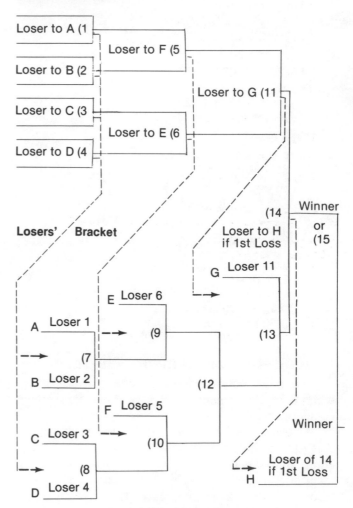

Court and Field Diagrams

Diagrams and dimensions of the following playing areas are included: basketball, volleyball, softball, soccer, tennis, badminton, one-wall paddleball, horseshoes, shuffleboard, and croquet.

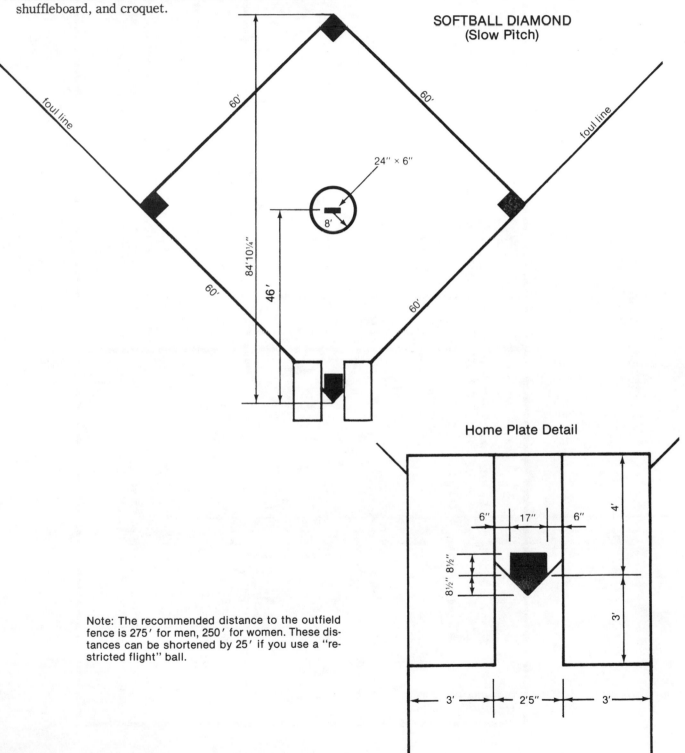

SOFTBALL DIAMOND
(Slow Pitch)

Home Plate Detail

Note: The recommended distance to the outfield fence is 275' for men, 250' for women. These distances can be shortened by 25' if you use a "restricted flight" ball.

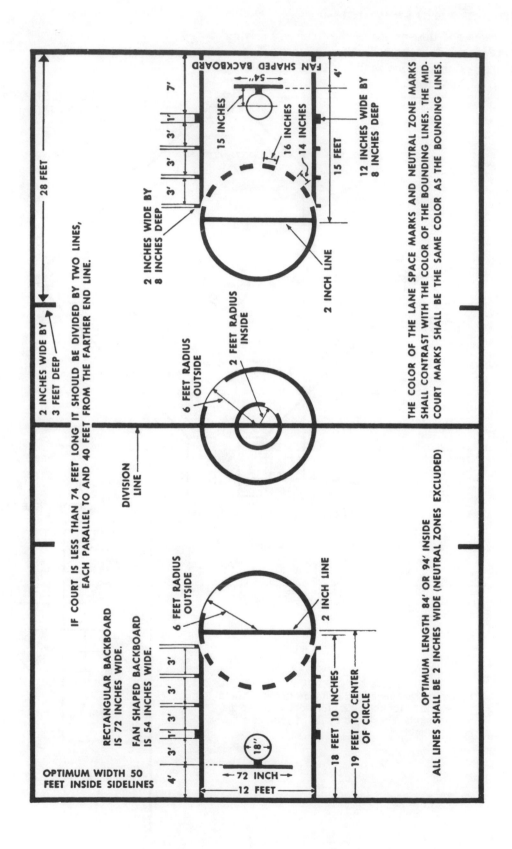

BASKETBALL COURT

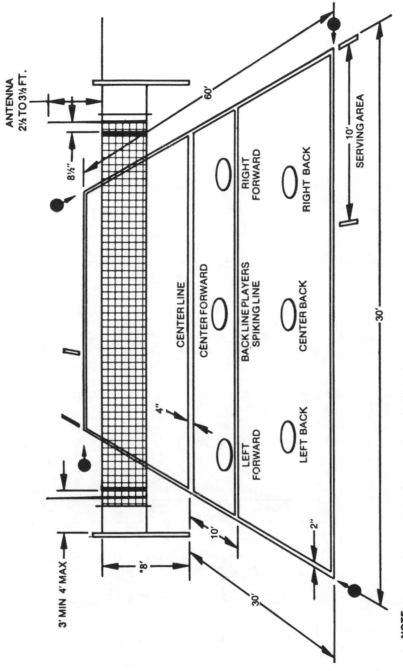

VOLLEYBALL COURT

NOTE
ALL LINES ARE 2" WIDE EXCEPT CENTER LINE WHICH IS 4 INCHES
*7 FEET 4¼ INCHES FOR WOMEN

● INDICATES POSITION OF LINESMAN WHEN FOUR ARE USED

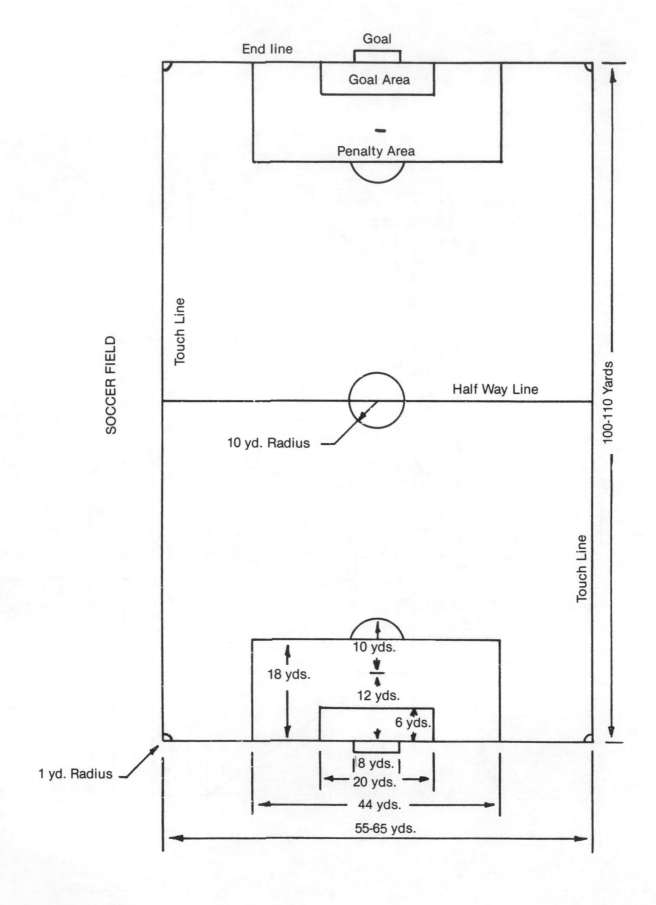

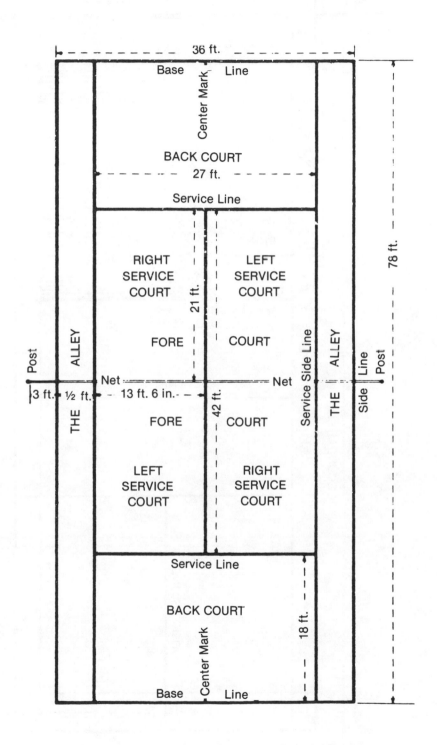

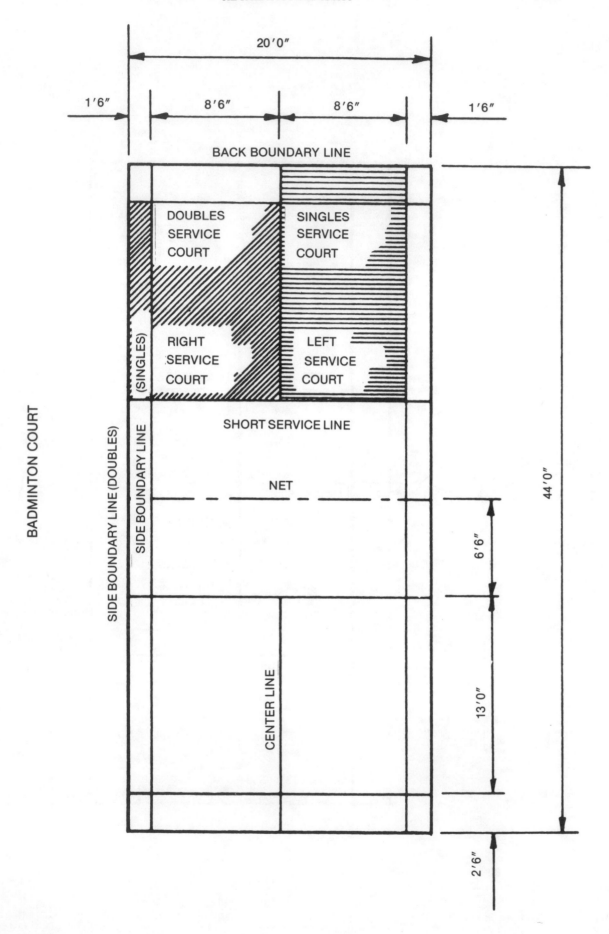

BADMINTON COURT

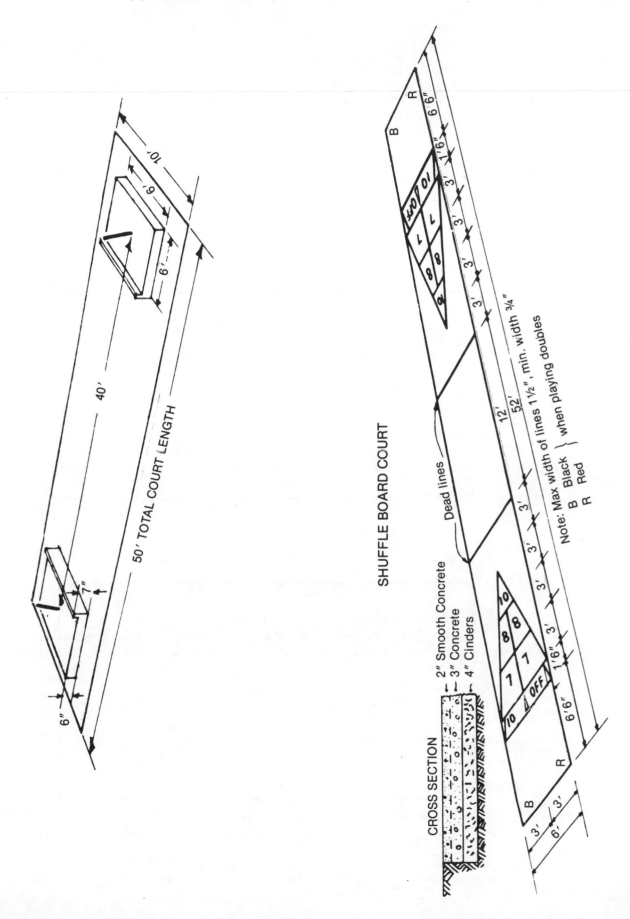

HORSESHOE COURT

10'

6'

6'

40'

50' TOTAL COURT LENGTH

7"

6"

SHUFFLE BOARD COURT

B R

6'6"

1'6"

3'

10 OFF

L

8

7

3'

3'

3'

3'

12'

52'

Dead lines

Note: Max width of lines 1½", min. width ¾"
B   Black } when playing doubles
R   Red

10
8 8
7 7
10 OFF
1'6" 3'
3'
3'
3'
6'6"
B R
3' 3'
3' 6'

CROSS SECTION

2" Smooth Concrete
3" Concrete
4" Cinders

ONE-WALL PADDLEBALL COURT

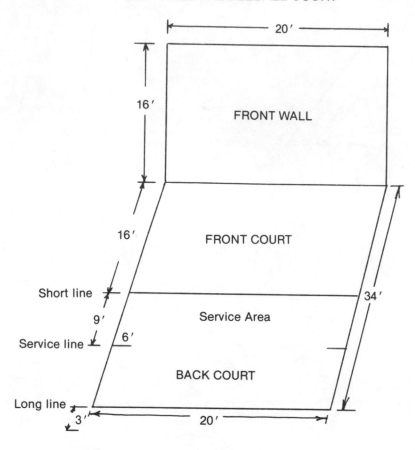

CROQUET COURT

CROQUET (AMERICAN). Court 30′ X 60′. Playing lines 2′ 6″ inside the boundary lines. Arches 4″ or less wide X 10″ high. First arch is 8′ from end boundary lines; second is 7′ in front of first; side arches in line with second arch are 5′ 9″ from side boundary lines (3′ 3″ from side playing lines). Arches may have round or square tops. (If double center arches are used, place at right angles to other arches, 18″ apart.)

INDEX